Dear Reader,

The book you are holding came about in a rather different way to most others. It was funded directly by readers through a new website: Unbound. Unbound is the creation of three writers. We started the company because we believed there had to be a better deal for both writers and readers. On the Unbound website, authors share the ideas for the books they want to write directly with readers. If enough of you support the book by pledging for it in advance, we produce a beautifully bound special subscribers' edition and distribute a regular edition and ebook wherever books are sold, in shops and online.

This new way of publishing is actually a very old idea (Samuel Johnson funded his dictionary this way). We're just using the internet to build each writer a network of patrons. At the back of this book, you'll find the names of all the people who made it happen.

Publishing in this way means readers are no longer just passive consumers of the books they buy, and authors are free to write the books they really want. They get a much fairer return too – half the profits their books generate, rather than a tiny percentage of the cover price.

If you're not yet a subscriber, we hope that you'll want to join our publishing revolution and have your name listed in one of our books in the future. To get you started, here is a £5 discount on your first pledge. Just visit unbound.com, make your pledge and type **annabel5** in the promo code box when you check out.

Thank you for your support,

Dan, Justin and John
Founders, Unbound

ANNABEL

VS

THE

INTERNET

Annabel Port

Unbound

This edition first published in 2018

Unbound
6th Floor Mutual House, 70 Conduit Street, London W1S 2GF
www.unbound.com

of this w ... Copyright,
Desig ... copied,
rep ... form
or b ... or be
othe ... hat in
whi ... osed

A ... ry

ISBN 978-1-78352-447-1 (trade tpb)
ISBN 978-1-78352-448-8 (ebook)
ISBN 978-1-78352-446-4 (limited edition)

Printed in Great Britain by Clays Ltd, St Ives Plc

1 3 5 7 9 8 6 4 2

For Mum and Dad

Contents

Introduction
(or why I started doing all this)

I'm in a London Underground train carriage, surrounded by complete strangers, sitting in complete silence. We are between stops and trapped together. Trapped together underground. And I'm silently willing myself to break the biggest unwritten rule of the Tube: don't talk.

I go to speak several times. I take a breath, and the words are ready. But I can't do it. My mouth just won't say them.

What is less welcome than a complete stranger on the London Underground, during the day – not even a drunken night, but during the day – turning to her fellow passengers and blurting out, "So, where's everyone going, then?"

I take another breath, then clap my hands together.

"So, where's everyone going, then?"

It is so excruciating that it's like I'm having an out-of-body experience. I hear the words as I say them, but I don't feel like they're coming from my mouth. And I have no idea why my hands did that clap.

The three people opposite look at me with great surprise. Then one, a man in a suit, says, "Work."

"Ooh. What do you do?"

He tells me he works in finance. He doesn't want to talk to

me. I can tell.

There's a girl to his right. I say, "Are you off to work too?'

She tells me, "I'm at work now."

This confuses me a bit as she's eating peanuts and reading a book and I'm not sure that's an actual profession, but I don't want to start a row so I leave it there.

There's a middle-aged man to my right who is stubbornly refusing to get involved, so I say to him, "Weather's terrible, isn't it?"

He ignores me. In case he's hard of hearing, I say it again.

"Is it?" he replies.

I say, "Yes, have you not been outside today?"

I realise there's a possibility that I might be starting to sound aggressive and we're pulling into a station so I decide it's time to get off.

I say, "Bye," and the peanut lady gives me a lovely smile. I see what I strongly suspect is relief on the faces of all the others.

It was never my aim to demolish the wall of social constraint. It was the unexpected consequence of a big push from my friend Geoff.

I was working as a waitress in a cocktail bar when I met Geoff. Which is true, but mostly irrelevant to the story. In addition to living out the lyrics of an iconic eighties pop song, I was also doing work experience at a radio station where Geoff was a presenter. In my first two weeks, I spent eight solid days stuffing envelopes. Clearly, something about the way I handled those envelopes suggested to Geoff that I wasn't achieving my full potential in life. I was also the first person he saw when his producer left suddenly and he urgently needed someone to answer the phones and make the tea on his evening show.

So I answered the phones and made the tea, and the evening show turned into a breakfast show, then a late-night show, then a drivetime show and somewhere along the way I'd become Geoff's co-presenter.

I still wasn't achieving my full potential in Geoff's eyes, though. He thought I was in a premature middle age. No, that's far too generous. A premature, deeply dull, very old age. The kind where you're propped up with pillows in an armchair all day. He was mostly right. I live in a cul-de-sac. I like to watch episodes of *Miss Marple*. Probably the wildest thing I ever do is take a Sainsbury's carrier bag to use in a Tesco supermarket. Very, very occasionally.

I'm also deeply lazy. I don't know if there's a lazy gene as I've never got round to googling it, but if there is, I've got it. When caught in the rain, it's not uncommon for me to get soaking wet because I can't be bothered to get my umbrella out of my bag. I did once summon the energy to paint the hallway of my flat, but it then took me another eight years to remove the masking tape. And that was only because I was moving out.

I haven't always led such a plodding, mundane, lazy life. Before radio, before the cocktail bar, I'd lived abroad for three years, in Poland, Portugal and Mexico. Think how worldly I must be, that I took my unexciting life from the UK and replicated it somewhere else thousands of miles away. I only went to avoid the effort of having to start a career.

I didn't stray too far from the towns where I worked as an English language teacher. On one occasion in Poland, egged on by the other teachers, I took a trip to Krakow. The morning we were due to visit Auschwitz, I kept pressing snooze and missed the bus. If I'd gone abroad to find myself, I'd found that I was a terrible person.

I ended up coming home because, besides my friends and family, I missed British television too much. At least now I knew what I was looking for in life: a good crime drama.

So I came home, got a job in a bar and then a job in radio, and the rest of the time just settled in front of the television.

It's understandable, then, why Geoff thinks I waste my life watching exciting things happen to other people. So he decided to set me various challenges, partly to give us something to talk about on the radio, partly for his own amusement, and partly with the belief that if he didn't keep me busy, I'd get sofa sores.

Sometimes my comfortable, boring life felt infinitely preferable. Sometimes I would find myself being escorted out of a building by a Herculean security guard and wonder why I'd chosen to accept these challenges. Sometimes I looked back on that excruciating time I spoke to complete strangers on the Tube as a comparatively halcyon day.

But I am a bit less lazy now. And I did right a terrible wrong from years earlier. One sad summer, my parents, feeling sorry for me, asked if they could take me on a summer holiday to cheer me up. I said yes, picturing beaches and cocktails. It was a trip to Auschwitz.

That moment of chatting to complete strangers on the London Underground opened up a whole new world to me. It was like a wall inside of me had been knocked down. A wall built from titanium that had previously stopped me from being able to do things like start a light conversation on public transport. I even did it again the very same day.

I'm now on a Tube train where three people, all in their late twenties, are talking to each other.

Covertly listening in, I hear one of them say, "They're charging 5p to print each copy."

Feeling this is my cue, I ask, "What are you printing?"

The lady who'd spoken looks at me with a face that is difficult to describe. Imagine someone 60% horrified, 20% shocked, 10% disgusted, 5% freaked out and 5% angry, then multiply the intensity of that expression by about four. Now have that face stare at you in silence for five seconds before it speaks and says, "No, we're not printing anything."

This is confusing, but I feel a need to somehow redeem this situation. "Oh, it's just that I know somewhere cheap," I say, while thinking, *Please don't ask me where, I don't know anywhere cheap, I just made that up, please don't ask me where.*

She doesn't, and it's very clear that my input in this conversation is no longer required.

People aren't always friendly. And I've learned that I'm really bad at small talk. But strangely, I'd actually started to enjoy myself, living life one centimetre closer to the edge than before.

Author's Note

The events described all took place sometime
between 2009 and 2014.

1

The Challenge:
To live without the Internet

Geoff thinks I'm a Luddite. I'm not. I've got no problem at all
with mechanical weaving looms. And I'm not a technophobe.
I own a mobile phone, digital camera, PlayStation 3, laptop,
Sky box and microwave. But while this is all very useful infor-
mation for anyone planning to burgle me, it doesn't convince
Geoff.

He feels that I'm not embracing the modern age, mainly
because I've not yet joined Twitter. He suspects I think we
were fine before all these newfangled things came along, so
why do we need them now? There may be some truth in
this.

He challenges me to find out if I'm right. To live without
the Internet and prove that it's not so great. That you can have
the same experience of all these different websites, without
ever going online. Then if a giant bug comes along and eats
the Internet, who cares? We'll all be just fine.

Part one: Celebrity gossip

I suspect that Tim Berners-Lee, when inventing the World Wide Web, didn't intend for it to be used for celebrity gossip. Or maybe he did. Maybe he only invented it so he could keep regular tabs on Noel Edmonds. But I'm sure I can find out some red-hot celebrity gossip without having to use hugely popular sites like Heatworld and Perez Hilton.

I begin at lunchtime in London and I know exactly where all the celebrities are. The Ivy. The restaurant tucked away down a side street with the annoyingly opaque windows so you can't see through to gawp at all the famous faces.

Obviously I've not got a table booked. That would've required a huge amount of forethought and an entry in the most recent *Who's Who*. I have neither.

But the last time I went to a restaurant, I told the waiter who greeted me that I was meeting someone there, and then just went through to find them.

Admittedly that was Pizza Express, but I see no reason why I can't do the same. Then I'll have a good wander about, check out the toilets and, after making a spurious excuse, leave.

I'm genuinely pleased with this plan, so when I arrive I walk in with confidence.

The first thing I see is a lady in a cloakroom. They don't have this at Pizza Express, but after giving the woman a smile intending to convey that I come here all the time and this is all perfectly normal, I pass through some more doors with purpose and find myself at the entrance to the dining area.

I can't yet see through to the sea of celebrities as my view is blocked to my right by a bar and to my left by a man, who if I were at Pizza Express would be a waiter. But I'm not; I'm at The Ivy. He's the maître d' and he's greeting me. I'm suddenly not sure it's going to be that easy to breeze past him to my imaginary friend.

I say with as much confidence as I can muster, "Hello, I'm meeting someone here. Can I just go through?"

"Yes, of course," he replies. Great, I think. Until he adds, "What's the name of the person you're meeting?"

This would be a good time to leave. I could feign amnesia or something that requires immediate medical attention. But not so immediate they need to dial 999. That would be a good thing to do. Instead I blurt out the first name that comes into my mind.

"Jo."

"And their surname?" the maître d' asks.

I could still get out of this. Amnesia is still an option.

"I'm not sure, actually, as it's a client."

I have never had a client in my life. I've only ever been a client myself at the hairdresser's. I don't know where this sentence has come from but it has now led the maître d' to say, "Right," and begin scanning the reservations book.

In my state of rising panic and silent prayers of, *Please don't let there be a Jo here. Please*, I've not forgotten the purpose of my visit. I have a really good look at the book to see if I can spot a famous person.

I notice a Davina. But it's not Davina McCall. I remind myself that celebrities don't always use their real names and keep an eye out for a Mickey Mouse or Donald Duck, but there's nothing.

These thoughts are interrupted by the maître d' saying,

"Oh, I've got a Jo Robinson. Is that who you're meeting?"

This is not good. Really not good. The right answer to this question would be no.

"Hmmm," I say. "Robinson doesn't ring a bell."

That should do the trick. I can be out of here in seconds.

But he has another question. "Was this arranged recently?"

"Erm, yes, I think it was yesterday."

"I think it must be this one. Okay, follow me."

Before I can make a last-ditch pretence of memory loss, I'm being whisked away and led through the restaurant. I'm in such an advanced stage of panic over what I'm going to do when taken to the table of this Jo Robinson, who I've never met before and is definitely not meeting me for lunch, that I don't even think to look around for celebrities.

I am sweating by the time we arrive at the table.

And it's an empty table. An empty table for two. Jo hasn't arrived yet. The relief is immense.

Within milliseconds, though, a waiter has appeared and is pulling a chair out for me to sit down, putting a menu in front of me and asking me what I'd like to drink.

I find myself saying, "I think I'll just wait for my client to arrive."

And I realise that a whole new horror has opened up to me. That Jo will eventually arrive and be shown to this table to find a complete stranger sitting there.

While I'm desperately thinking what to do next, I do take a few seconds to have a good look around me at all the celebrities. I'm not going through all this humiliation without some reward. I want to see Kate Moss playing footsie with Robert Mugabe, or Jude Law sharing a table, laid for two, with a teddy bear.

I don't see this though. I see nothing. Not one celebrity.

The waiter is now bringing me a bread basket and a paper to read and I can endure this no longer.

I get up and head back towards the exit. I pass by the maître d', who gives me a questioning look.

"I just checked my phone and realised I'm in the wrong place." I tell him. "We're meeting at Pizza Express."

Internet 1, Annabel 0.

Part two: eBay

eBay is next. To emulate this, I need to sell some things I don't want any more for the very best price. I go round my flat, looking for what I can turn into cold, hard cash.

In the kitchen, I find a Jamie Oliver Flavour Shaker, best described as a less effective pestle and mortar. I got it one Christmas, used it twice and then never touched it again. I brush the dust off and notice it's got Jamie's name on it, which is good as an autograph, so I can say it's signed.

Next I see a Wonder Woman figurine that's been lying about for ages. I've almost put it in a bag destined for the charity shop three times now, but felt guilty as it was a gift. I was given it at the end of a job I did a few years ago. (They paid me as well.)

I look through a pile of vinyl that I rarely play and find the 12-inch of Northside's "Shall We Take a Trip". There's also an album called *Chart Hits 81*, featuring the "Birdie Song", Ottowan's "Hands Up" and "Can Can" by Bad Manners. As I don't subscribe to *Record Collector* magazine, I have no idea if these are now very rare and valuable. I presume they are.

These go in my carrier bag too.

Now I've got all my goods. I just need to decide how and where to sell them. As eBay is an auction site, perhaps the best non-Internet alternative is an auction house. The only one I can think of is Sotheby's, which is good since I've got an "in" there. My cousin Belinda once did work experience there for two weeks, eighteen years ago.

I head off down New Bond Street to Sotheby's, where there's a man in a fancy suit on the door. He asks if I'm okay. "Just got some things to sell," I say, holding up my Tesco carrier bag and then breeze past him. He doesn't stop me.

I go to reception and tell the woman that I'm here to sell. She sends me straight up to the valuation counter. It's that easy. I didn't even know that there was a such a thing as a valuation counter. I'd assumed all this kind of thing was done in opulent hotel rooms or bank vaults. I haven't even needed to mention my cousin Belinda yet.

I walk down the hall and up the stairs to my left. It's all bouncy carpets and cream walls. I reach the valuation counter and tell the woman I've got some goods to auction and start pulling the things out of my carrier bag. She is very polite but says they wouldn't be able to do the Jamie Oliver Flavour Shaker, the Northside single, the eighties album or the Wonder Woman toy. They only sell paintings, sculpture and jewellery.

I ask if she can give me a rough valuation so that wherever I go next, I can say I got my things valued at Sotheby's. She's afraid not. Not even the Flavour Shaker. She probably got egg on her face once by undervaluing an Antony Worrall Thompson Electric Knife.

She does tell me though, that Bonhams auction toys, so I

should try there. They are just down the road, so off I go.

There's no one on the door this time, so I go straight to reception and explain again that I'm here to sell. The woman agrees to take a look.

I show her the Flavour Shaker first. I make sure I point out that it's signed this time. She says that it's still very modern but she thinks maybe it'll be worth something in a few years. I press her to say how many years. She says about five. I make a mental note to bring it back then.

Next I show her the vinyl. She has to ring the entertainment section for an answer on this. She must need a second opinion. This is good. I listen in as she says in a very well-spoken voice, "I've got here Northside and 'Shall We Take a Trip.'"

I whisper that it's a double-A side with "Moody Places". I hear her say, "No, it's not signed." I wished I'd signed it now. And known the name of anyone in Northside.

Then she tries *Chart Hits 81*. I whisper to her, "Some of the artists might be dead, if that helps."

Unfortunately, the person on the other end of the line is not interested if they're not signed and has never heard of Northside. Where was he in 1990?

I try the Wonder Woman toy last. She now has to ring the toy department. She doesn't say much on the phone this time and doesn't speak for very long. She puts the phone down and says to me, "They've given an estimate of £80 to £120."

It's the most amazing moment. £80 to £120! If it had happened on *Antiques Roadshow*, the clip would've been shown for years to come. I can't believe I'd nearly given it to charity three times.

The only drawback is that the next toy auction is four months away. But I'm really buoyed and am now determined to get rid of the records and the Flavour Shaker.

I go to Habitat. Habitat has got to be buzzing with kitchen-gadget-loving people. I approach around thirty of them with, "Would you like to buy a Jamie Oliver Flavour Shaker?" Not one person is interested. I start feeling like I'm in an episode of *The Apprentice* but I'm one of the really awful, useless contestants, who don't get fired straight away, as their idiocy and incompetence is making good television.

I decide to give it one last try with the records. I go to the Music and Video Exchange in Soho. The man says, "I can give you, let's see . . ."

I wait excitedly.

"I can give you 25p."

I'm not selling my records for 25p.

I've still got the records and Flavour Shaker, but a £80–120 estimate on my Wonder Woman toy. I've just got to go back in four months. I do wonder if eBay is not slightly quicker. But in Annabel vs the Internet, I'm calling it a draw.

Part three: Facebook

Why can't I have a non-Internet Facebook page? What would be so strange about that? What's the difference between having one on the Internet and having one on a piece of paper that you carry around with you? I suspect I'll have to find the answer to all these questions myself.

I start by trying to find some old work friends, which Facebook is often used for. I go back through my old jobs and count twenty-four of them. I had twenty-three of these between the ages of twelve and twenty-five. Starting with my paper round, which I did from the illegal age of twelve to the weirdly old age of eighteen.

The problem is that a lot of the places I worked don't exist any more, and I'm struggling to remember the names of anyone in the other places.

A more recent job was from nine years ago when I worked as a staffroom assistant at an English language school in London. It's not far from where I work now, so I decide to go down there as I'm better with faces than names.

First, I quickly make my non-Internet Facebook page. I tear a piece of paper from my A5 notebook and write FACE-BOOK at the top. Then I draw a box round it to jazz it up a bit. I need a profile picture, so in the top right-hand corner I do a quick sketch of myself, adding some defined cheekbones and long eyelashes that I don't have in real life. Next I write my name *Annabel Port* and then *Friends*. Then there is a lot of blank space.

I'm starting to get little worried: working at an English language school can be quite a transient job, so everyone I was friends with at the time has probably left. But when I get there, I immediately recognise someone. A woman, whose name I think is Anne. She works on reception and I'd see her every day. We'd sometimes have a little chat. She's the sort of person where it's almost impossible to guess her age with any confidence.

"Hello! Is it Anne?" I say. I'm really hoping it is Anne.

"Yes," she says. I can tell straight away that she has no idea who I am.

"Do you remember me? I used to work here."

Anne looks surprised and a bit embarrassed. "Oh, no, I don't."

"It's Annabel. I was the staffroom assistant. We worked together."

"No, sorry. I'm really sorry."

She's very apologetic but I'm actually quite insulted. I worked there for eight months. I saw her every workday for eight months. I sometimes used to cover reception for her. It was only nine years ago. I recognised her straight away. But I refuse to let the fact she doesn't know who I am get in the way of making a Facebook friend.

I say, "Well, the reason I'm here is I've set up a Facebook page, except not on the Internet." I show her my page, then continue with, "And I was looking for old friends to contact and so I'd like to request your friendship."

I'm thinking now, *Okay she doesn't remember me, but all she's got to do is write her name on a bit of paper.*

"Oh . . . no, I won't," she says.

I'm a little surprised.

"All you've got to do is write your name here and perhaps draw a little picture of yourself or I could draw it."

"No, it's not for me. Maybe you'd like to ask someone else here you used to work with."

"Well, you're the person I most remember." This is a lie. I barely knew her.

"No, I'm really sorry."

She doesn't want to do it so much that she won't even write her name just to get rid of me. She could just scribble something indecipherable. But she won't.

I'm getting desperate so I say, "I'll be honest with you, Anne. I'm quite hurt. You were the first person I thought of and the first person I asked."

It doesn't make the slightest bit of difference and actually I think she's getting a little freaked out now.

So I leave, saying, "It's been great catching up." Another lie.

It's going very badly. But I realise something. You look at some people's pages and they've got over five hundred friends. They can't know all of those people well. They're people they've just met. This is the way to get Facebook friends.

I get on the London Underground. A Japanese girl is sitting next to me reading a free newspaper. After a couple of stops I turn to her and say, "I'm getting off at the next stop so just wanted to say it's been really nice sitting next to you."

She doesn't reply but smiles in a really nice way.

I carry on, "So I was wondering if I could request your friendship." I show her my Facebook page.

She laughs out loud at me and then says, "Oh no, no, no."

At my Tube stop there's a WHSmith in the station. I buy some chewing gum and while the man is serving me I say, "How's your day going?"

He replies, "Good, thanks," but I get the impression he's not used to actually talking to customers.

When the transaction is finished, I say, "Now we've met and had a nice chat, could I request your friendship on my Facebook page?"

"Oh, okay," he says and takes my Facebook page and writes his name.

I tell him that he can either draw a picture of his own face or I'll do it for him. He says I can. So I do. There's a bit of a queue building behind me. He doesn't seem bothered, so I take my time. When I finish, he says, "Thanks ma'am," like I'm the Queen. Even though I realise later that my picture looks like if you'd asked a five-year-old to draw a Chinese person without eyeballs. And he wasn't Chinese. But he didn't seem to mind at all. This is going great.

I've got my first friend! I'm ready to meet more new people.

I start walking from Oxford Street down to Piccadilly Circus. There's a road full of those charity clipboard people who always approach me. I've tried pretending to be on the phone and pretending to cry. Neither work. I'm currently signed up to five of them. They owe me.

What I'm thinking is, *If they stop me, we've met, so I can ask them to be my friend.*

I walk down the road and not one of them approaches me. Not one. I'm even making eye contact with them and at one stage looking pleadingly at both them and the clipboard. Not one stops me. Unbelievable.

I need to try something different to make friends. I see a man and say, "Excuse me, which way is Carnaby Street?" He tells me, then as he's walking off I say, "It's been really good talking to you, can I request your friendship?"

"Oh, okay," he says. He even looks a bit pleased. He writes his name, Terry, and I draw a picture of him.

"How shall I say I know you?" I ask him.

"Why don't you write that we met walking down Argyll Street?"

"And can I have your telephone number so I can ring you to give you my status updates?"

He agrees and writes it down.

"What about your address?" I ask now. "If you write that down I can come and write on your wall."

It's one step too far. But I won't let him leave without me giving him a little Facebook poke on the arm.

Apart from making Facebook friends, I'm picking up my new iPhone today. I'm in the Orange shop with an assistant called Adam and going through the serious business of setting up my new tariff, signing contracts, etc.

Towards the end I say, "Well, it's been great spending time with you. I feel like we're friends now."

He looks worried.

"Would you be my friend on Facebook?" I ask.

"I'm not on Facebook."

"No I mean this one." And I show him my page.

He looks even more worried now but he lets me write his name. I draw his picture and then say, "And if I want to send you a cupcake or throw a sheep at you, shall I just come to this shop?"

Adam agrees that would be the best thing to do. He's probably relieved I haven't suggested coming to his house.

I leave feeling happy. I've got four friends. Then an hour or so later, I remember that I'd promised to give Terry, who I met on Argyll Street, my status updates. I ring the number that he gave me. It rings and then goes to a voicemail saying the person is unavailable. Then the line goes straight from that message to a ringing tone again. I stay on the line. There's no answer, just the message again and then the ringing tone again and so on.

On about the fifth time I've continually rung his number,

Terry answers. I say, "Hi, it's Annabel. Your Facebook friend."

He sounds uncomfortable and says, "I'm in class at the moment so I can't really talk."

"Oh, what are you studying?"

He tells me he's at printing college.

"Well, I just wanted to give you my status update. Annabel is happy because a man called her ma'am like you would the Queen."

"Oh, okay, well I can't talk now."

"Fine," I say. "I'll ring you later."

I don't, as he's probably changed his number. But I do really feel like I managed to recreate the whole experience of Facebook with my own piece of paper.

I think it's very clear that on this occasion, it's Internet 0, Annabel 1.

Final score: Annabel 2, Internet 1. Let that giant bug do its worst – we can easily live without the Internet. So long as we are also prepared to live without our dignity.

2

The Challenge: To prove that Britain isn't broken

The tabloid newspapers are telling us that we are living in Broken Britain. That teenagers are out of control, women are behaving worse than ever before, we're all spongers, there's endless anti-social behaviour and the country is basically unrecognisable as the great place it used to be. But are they right? Is it really broken? Geoff challenges me to find out.

Part one: Teenagers

I start with teenagers. Teenagers today get a bad press. If I believed everything I've read, they are all, right now, in a WKD Blue and Miaow Miaow-fuelled orgy of simultaneously stabbing each other and contracting chlamydia. While playing music loudly on their mobile phones.

Actually, that last bit is probably true. That's one thing

I can confirm from my extremely limited interaction with teenagers.

On one occasion, when faced with the loud, tinny and bad music from a mobile, I asked the owner to turn it down and he didn't thrust a screwdriver into my eye socket. No. He smiled and then turned it down. A tiny bit.

I already have my doubts that adolescents are playing any role in the breaking of Britain, if it is going on.

Perhaps, though, this one encounter isn't enough to make my findings statistically significant. I think Pavlov, for example, tried his response thing out on more than one dog. I need to get among the teens.

One place I know I won't be able to find them is at school. Not because they're all bunking off for that stabbing/chlamydia orgy. No, because it's half term.

This knowledge comes with some relief. I hadn't fancied hanging around any school gates for reasons that would be even more obvious if I were a middle-aged man.

However, my relief is soon tainted by the realisation that I have absolutely no idea what teenagers do in half term.

One thought does eventually strike me: Youth clubs. I never went to one when I was younger but I've seen *Byker Grove* on the telly so I know teenagers go there. And blind themselves with paintball guns.

I'm not thrilled by the prospect. I toy briefly with the idea of wearing some kind of safety goggle. But with Donal MacIntyre-like abandon, I venture to a youth club I'd found on the Internet, not too far from where I live in east London.

As I'm making my way there, I start thinking about how to befriend these teenagers and I decide my best bet is to pretend I'm one of them. Despite the fact I'm in my mid-thirties.

But just last year I got asked for ID when buying wine in Tesco, even though I was also buying sweet potatoes and a product from the Tesco Finest range, and what teenager buys goods from the Tesco Finest range? Maybe Brooklyn Beckham. But that's it. I might just get away with it.

It's a horrible day, pouring with rain, so I'm wet and cold when I arrive at the youth club. I go in. It's a room with a snooker table, pool table and table tennis table. My first thought is: teenagers really like table-based ball sports.

Next, I notice the people. There are five teenage boys, one teenage girl and an old lady sitting on a chair. I'm really pleased to see her. Because if she's getting away with masquerading as a teenager, then this is going to be a breeze for me.

As I walk in, one of the boys greets me with a gruff, "What do you want?"

It's not a great welcome.

"Just to hang out," I tell him.

He says something a bit grunty and points towards another room, where I see what must be the youth-club leader. He's painting a wall mural. I'm not getting real life confused with an episode of *Byker Grove* again. He really is painting a wall mural.

I approach him saying, "Hello, what's the age range here?"

I don't want to go too high with my fake teenager age. He tells me it's thirteen to nineteen but they take them from eleven during half term.

He then adds, "How old are your kids?"

This is disastrous. Not only do I not look teenage, I clearly look old enough to have teenage children. Which, actually, I am. Easily. But I'm not giving up.

"Oh no, it's for me," I say.

"Oh, how old are you?" he asks.

"Seventeen."

I probably should've said nineteen. I have no idea why I didn't. I could've been two teenage years older. I suspect some kind of pathetic defiance was involved here. But he just looks a bit surprised and then responds with, "Okay, no problem."

He's probably thinking, quite rightly, *Why would anyone lie about their age to go in a room and sit and watch a handful of teenagers play table-based ball sports?*

I go back into the main room and sit and watch a handful of teenagers play table-based ball sports. I can't see any violence or transference of pelvic inflammatory disease, but maybe they're being discreet. I need to interact.

The sole other girl is also sitting down and I overhear her call her mum and ask her to come and pick her up.

At this stage, I too want to call my mum and ask her to come and pick me up.

This is a girl I'd normally be too scared even to speak to. She has blonde hair in a very strange ponytail that forms a fan shape on top of her head. She's wearing a lot of gold jewellery. Less than Mr T but more than your average rapper. Obviously, I don't mention this, mainly as there's no way she'll know who Mr T is.

Instead, I force myself to ask her if she wants to play table tennis with me. She mumbles something about not knowing how and I must look really dejected because she says, "Oh, okay then."

We're playing table tennis. I'm a bit distracted at first. I start to worry that the youth-club leader will come over and ask for my date of birth. I'm trying to work it out but I keep coming up with 1994, which can't be right as 1994 was yesterday.

When I finally come to terms with it, I start trying to make some conversation. It doesn't go very well.

Firstly, I find out her age. She's eighteen. This is older than I thought and it also means that I'm pretending to be younger than her.

Then I delve further by asking, "Do you live round here?" and she replies, "Just moved here."

The table tennis is going well, though. We laugh when I really miss the ball, which happens quite a lot. She's better than me, which makes me realise she'd lied a bit about not knowing how to play. Maybe lying a bit is the start of a slippery slope into gonorrhoea. What if she's about to offer me Class A drugs?

She doesn't. She's just polite and as friendly to a mid-thirty-something pretending to be a seventeen-year-old in a youth club as you could possibly hope anyone to be.

I eventually decide to leave before the youth-club leader asks me for my birth certificate. I say goodbye to my new friend. I walk out of that youth club alive, and I'm pretty sure I didn't catch any STDs.

Part two: Ladettes

It's time for the ladettes to come under my scrutiny now.

These ladettes, or women behaving badly, are most commonly depicted as rolling around drunk, and I have noticed a big increase in this recently. Not in real life, but in pictures in the paper. Even though I tend to think that if something is news, it's because it's unusual and not an everyday occurrence.

I check the latest figures for women and drinking at the

Official National Statistics website and learn that the peak of women binge drinking was between 1998–2002 but it dropped after that. And women are still drinking substantially less than men.

I decide to see how many ladies I can spot behaving badly on the way to work. In the thirty minutes it takes me to go on my journey from east to central London, I see nothing. Maybe it's a quiet day for the ladette, maybe something to do with the weather. But I'm sure I could persuade some girls to behave badly and then deny it's entrapment.

I'm on the escalator coming out of the Tube station. There's a girl in front of me. I tap her on the shoulder and she turns round. She's a pretty blonde and she smiles at me.

I say, "Excuse me, do you want to flash your boobs with me at the people on the other escalator?"

She looks stunned. And then starts laughing.

"Are you serious?" she asks.

I tell her I am.

"Why?" she asks.

"It'll be fun," I say.

"No! We'll both be sent to jail."

I'm not sure about jail, unless we do it in Saudi Arabia, and that wasn't the plan. I move on. I'm outside on the street walking through London's seedy Soho.

I go up to another lady and say, "Excuse me but would you like to happy slap me?"

She doesn't understand "happy slapping", so I explain that she beats me up, films it on her mobile and she can upload it onto the Internet.

"Oh," the lady says. "No, I don't want to."

I ask another woman. She, too, has never heard of it. I

explain again. She also doesn't want to, but adds, "Cheers anyway." This is very polite. I don't understand it. Why isn't she screaming at me then smashing a bottle of Diamond White in my face?

I try something different. I approach a couple of girls together and say, "Excuse me, do you want to come binge drinking with me and then pass out on the pavement with our bits on display?"

The answer is, "Not especially," which is not a definite no. This is progress.

I think back to all the sensationalist pictures of drunk women in the papers. One I immediately think of is that lady in Cardiff city centre with knickers round her ankles. Even though it turned out they weren't actually her knickers. And that she wasn't drunk.

I Google Image search "women drunk" and I find an article from the *Sun* called "New Year's Heaven" and there are seven photos of people lying about drunk, five of whom are women. Every single one of these women have amazing legs and all are in really short skirts.

I start wondering if binge drinking among women really is a problem, or just an excuse to print pictures of girls with their skirts riding up.

I have an idea. I call up the *Sun* news desk. A stressed-sounding man answers.

"Hello. I've got a story for you. I'm looking out of the window in central London and there is a lady, in broad daylight, rolling around drunk. She's in jeans and a jumper and is just lolling all over the pavement. Will you send a photographer down?"

"Well, we're in Wapping so they might be gone by the time someone gets there. Can you video it yourself?"

He doesn't seem particularly interested, so I add, "Oh! I can see another girl now rolling around. She's in a really short skirt and has got bare legs in this weather. Really nice legs."

I might be wrong but I feel he definitely perks up. "Can you get someone to video it and then call me back?"

"Will you put it in the paper?" I ask.

He tells me it depends on the quality, so I should film it, call him back and then we'll discuss remuneration.

I'm liking "remuneration". I beg him to tell me how much I'll get. It's around £200, depending on the quality and what they do with it.

I am now so tempted to go outside and do some serious lolling about in a short skirt while someone films it. Two hundred pounds! Is this the cause of the ladette culture? Then I remember my unshaven, bandy legs. And feminist principles. The temptation fades. Two hundred pounds is a lot, but it's still £50 less than you'd get for a *You've Been Framed* video.

Part three: Anti-social behaviour

Are the streets really heaving with anti-social behaviour? What even is anti-social behaviour? I find a Home Office report from 2004 that identified sixteen areas, including littering, noisy neighbours, fireworks, graffiti and insulting, pestering or intimidating behaviour.

They found that three-quarters of people asked had experienced a problem in one or more of these sixteen areas.

This is astonishing! Only three-quarters have experienced anti-social behaviour? Are one in four people hermits?

I've experienced seven out of sixteen. But not on a daily basis and it's surely not a new thing. In medieval times, people threw toilet waste out of the window. Things must be better now.

I need to see for myself how much of a problem anti-social behaviour is, and go out in search of it. I see a bit of litter on the ground on the way to the Tube. I'm not exactly wading through it, though. On the Tube map, above the station Shepherd's Bush, somebody has written in pen "The" before it. I think this person is just enriching society. But maybe I'm puerile.

Everybody is well behaved on my carriage. It wasn't like a few weeks ago when a man sat down and the lady next to him said, "No. Your legs are too wide open. You've got to close them."

Once in central London, I have a good long walk around the streets. I don't witness even one tiny bit of anti-social behaviour. Not even one litter drop. But I know it exists. We're told it exists. I'll just have to try and lure it in.

First thing I do is go and stand by a bin. I wait until someone approaches with some litter. The first person that does has a small paper cup to throw away. I stop her and say, "I dare you to throw that on the floor and not in the bin."

"Why would I do that?" she asks.

"It's a dare."

"No, I'm not going to do that dare," she says firmly and entirely reasonably.

Four more people said no. One added, "It's a good idea, though," which is one of the politest things I've ever heard.

I'm not having any success, so I say to the next person, "I'll give you 50p if you throw that plastic bottle on the floor."

He's quite keen. "Really? 50p?"

I start getting my purse out but his conscience gets the better of him. "Sorry, I can't do it. I can't take your money," he says and puts the bottle in the bin.

I can't even pay people to litter the streets.

I try another anti-social behaviour. Graffiti. I stand by a wall with a biro and stop passers-by, saying, "Hey, do you want to do some graffiti with me on this wall? We could write our names."

The first person says, "No thank you," adding as he walks off, "You're a weird one."

Two more politely say they don't fancy it. The fourth seems interested, in that he says, "Will it work?"

He has a point. I've picked a brick wall of an office building. I do an experimental mark with my biro on the cement bit. I just kind of scratch it. He's lost interest by now though and says he is late for something.

I try one more person, who says, "No, but only because I work in that building."

I still haven't lured anyone into anti-social behaviour. Surely I'll be able to find some insulting, pestering or intimidating behaviour, though. This one should be easy.

A man is sitting down outside a cafe.

I ask him, "Would you like to insult or intimidate me?"

"No, why would I do that?"

"Let off a bit of steam?" I suggest.

"No, thank you."

I ask two men standing together. They also don't want to. One of them adds, "But thanks for the opportunity."

Another two people don't want to say anything bad to me.

Outside a pub, I see three men. I approach them. As I do, they smile. I say, "Excuse me but would any of you like to insult or intimidate me?"

One of them says straight away, "Yes, bitch."

His two friends look horrified. It's like they've seen a side to him previously hidden. The bad man is laughing now. I don't think he meant it. But I'm worried that the other two will stop meeting him for a drink at lunchtime and start ignoring his calls.

I think I might have broken his Britain, but as for the rest of it, it appears very much intact. To the extent I'm starting to think we're actually a bunch of goody two shoes and we should start smashing it up and breaking society into bits. Then I remember the kind of clothes that anarchists wear and decide I prefer it this way. Living in an Unbroken Britain.

3

The Challenge: To tackle the
problems of the world economy

Experts are predicting that the world is on the brink of another global recession. Fortunately, Geoff has the answer.

Geoff: "I think a good thing for you to do would be to save the world economy."

Me: "Me?"

Geoff: "Yeah! Why not?"

There are many reasons why not. I'm briefly buoyed by the memory of my economics GCSE. Then I remember it was home economics. And, actually, just textiles. And I only got a C, even though my mum did all my sewing coursework for me.

I'm no expert, but off the top of my head, the best solution I can come up with is to get rid of money entirely.

Money is just fiction anyway. Most of it is just numbers being passed around by computers. The inhabitants of Yap, an island in South Pacific, use huge stone discs as money.

The biggest ones were made on an island 250 miles away and transported by boat. One day, the boat capsized and a really big disc fell to the bottom of the ocean. However, they still continued to use it as currency. They just kept transferring ownership of this disc at the bottom of the sea.

It seems like madness. But it's actually no different to how we use our money. Maybe we should be looking at alternatives.

My first idea is the barter system. There's a book about a man who started with a red paperclip and traded up over the course of a year to a house. I could try it out. It wouldn't really help the world economy but I'd be mortgage-free, so who cares!

I collect up a few things from around my flat that I don't want or need any more. By the end I have:

- A shower radio
- Two books. *Room* by Emma Donoghue and Stef Penney's *The Tenderness of Wolves*
- A DVD game of *Deal or No Deal*
- A risotto ai funghi sauce that I got free with an Ocado order
- The Rare Tea company's White Silver Tip Tea
- A corkscrew
- A pocket-size book called *The Life and Times of Hitler*
- A bottle of Dubonnet (A favourite of the Queen Mum. She loved gin and Dubonnet)
- A Clinique lipstick in Extreme Pink

I pack it all into a bag. Then come across my first problem. It's very heavy. I take out the bottle of Dubonnet. It's unlikely that I'm going be doing any swapping with the Queen Mum.

The bag is more manageable now. I'm ready to get bartering.

The best place to start is where something like £8 in every £10 is spent on the high street: Tesco. If I can persuade them to barter with me, I've practically changed the world economy in one step.

I need to buy some chillies so I take some to the till and put them down. I let the cashier know that I don't have any money and want to do a swap instead. I start pulling my barter goods out of the bag.

Once she ascertains that I didn't buy any of them at Tesco, she says she can't do anything but suggests I try customer services. I'm not massively surprised. I haven't ever seen any advertising indicating that they do swaps so I'm not hopeful that customer services will see this situation any differently.

There are two staff members there. One is serving, the other is pretending to be very busy with a calculator. I interrupt him by saying, "Shall I show you how to write the word boobless upside down on the calculator?"

He's keen to find out. I show him and he seems really pleased with this, despite the fact he's a man in his thirties.

I've really broken the ice, so I now go in with the swapping request, but he's not having any of it. It's a very firm no. He doesn't even seem to need to think about it. I can't persuade him. Not even with an offer to show him how to write "shoe-sole" on his calculator.

I give up and go to a newsagent to try and barter for some chewing gum. The lady waits until I've got everything out of my bag then says slowly, "I don't want any of it."

I move on and try and swap my stuff for a Twirl in another newsagent. I'm told the boss doesn't allow it. Like this happens a lot.

I'm in a small cafe and cake shop now and I'm really fed up. I say to the lady at the counter, "Can I swap some of this stuff in my bag for a cake?"

"Oh. What have you got?" she asks.

I let her have a good look. She checks the colour of the lipstick. She asks her colleague if she wants anything. She seems very interested in the *Deal or No Deal* game DVD. She takes one of the books as well, then asks, "How many cakes do you want?"

I say just one would be great.

"You can't just have one!"

I leave with two, feeling very cheered. The barter system is possible. Even though carrying around this big bag of stuff is pretty annoying. And one swap probably won't save the world economy. To make some more progress I need to turn to some other economic theories for inspiration.

I start looking on Wikipedia. Then I switch to Simple English Wikipedia. The basic version for people just starting to learn English and the simple-minded. I'm still struggling a bit. But I come across the Labour theory of value. Simplified, if it takes twice as long to make a table than a chair, you should pay twice as much for a table than a chair.

Great. I'll only pay for what goods are worth in terms of hours of labour. I decide that one hour will be worth £10, as it's a nice round number. It works out at about 16p per minute.

I go to a shop that just sells cookies and say to the man serving, "How long did it take to make that white chocolate chunk cookie?"

"Four days," he tells me.

I'm horrified. I'm never going to be able to afford it. It'll cost nearly a grand.

"Four days?" I say. "To make one cookie?"

He'd thought I'd asked how long I could keep it for. He has a better answer for how long it takes to prepare: thirteen minutes.

I get my calculator out and input the numbers, while trying to ignore the queue building behind me.

"Okay," I say once I've finished, "I'll pay you £2.08 for it."

He looks confused. I tell him I'm paying 16p per minute of labour.

"But they're priced by weight," he says.

"Well, I'm only paying £2.08," I tell him. "But we can weigh it if you want."

He does want to. He weighs it. "£1.30," he tells me firmly.

"Well, I'm afraid I'm still going to have to pay £2.08 for it." I give him a £20 note.

He is very confused. Perhaps understandably. "I can't do that," he says. He's starting to look a bit stressed.

I notice a tips jar by the till. "Okay," I tell him. "Give me whatever change you want and I'll put the extra seventy-eight pence that I need to pay in the tip jar."

This appears to satisfy him. I pay £2.08 for a £1.30 biscuit. I'm not 100% convinced this is the answer to the world economic problems. So far, it's just involved a very expensive biscuit.

I need to make more of an impact on the world economy. I'm thinking about the countries in particular difficulty. In Europe, Greece is probably in the worst state.

It seems sad that they've got such economic problems when they are home to the Acropolis. It's really old and famous; it must be worth a fortune. They should sell it like that time someone sold London Bridge to a rich American.

Then, I remember the Elgin Marbles. The Ancient Greek marble sculptures that the UK basically stole from Greece. If Greece had them back again, they could sell them.

I know we're not going to just give them back, though. They asked and we said no because we think they're not going to look after them properly. Presumably assuming they'll be smearing them in feta and spilling ouzo on them.

But what if the British Museum could be persuaded to sell them to someone and they then secretly gave them to Greece? This is the answer! I don't know who is going to buy them as I'm pretty sure I can't afford them, but I've decided to worry about that later and set about getting the museum to agree to sell them first.

I formulate a plan. Then ring up the British Museum main switchboard. A man answers.

"Hello, my name's Annabel. I'm a broker representing a client, who would like to remain anonymous at this time, and they would like to make a purchase."

He's a bit confused. "They want to buy something? What do they want to buy?"

"I'm not able to say at this time." I'm not sure why I said that; it just seemed professional to be discreet.

"Is it something in the museum?" the man asks.

I pause dramatically, then say solemnly, "Yes, that is correct."

He tells me that you can't buy things in the museum, which

isn't good, but then he adds, "I'll put you through to someone who might be able to help you."

I've passed the first hurdle! I'm getting closer to buying the Elgin Marbles for a currently non-existent client.

I'm being put through to a woman in the development department. I say to her, "I'm a broker representing a client who wishes to remain anonymous at present, but for the purposes of what I'm about to tell you, they are a worldwide name with considerable wealth."

She sounds excited. "Good!" she says.

I carry on. "And they want to make a purchase."

"Okay," she says.

"And the object in question is the Elgin Marbles."

She laughs a little. "Right!" she says. "Well, it's a bit of a sticky one. We're not legally allowed to sell objects. I'll have to get my director to call you. They're not going to be for sale but it's best if she speaks to you."

She goes on to say that the legal department can send me documents showing they can't sell the Elgin Marbles. I'm wondering how many offers they get that there are documents already drawn up.

But this is just the final hurdle to go over. Once I get the call from the director, I'm there. I've done it.

I wait for the call. It never comes. I'm very annoyed until I remember the buyer I was brokering for is imaginary.

And if they won't sell the Elgin Marbles, I'll just find some other way to get them. I'll just have to steal them. I don't feel bad about this. They were stolen by us in the first place and even named after the man that stole them, Mr Elgin, which would be regarded as foolish in any other kind of thievery situation. Maybe when I've got them, though, I'll rename them the Port Marbles.

I make my way to British Museum. I know this isn't going to be easy, but I'm thinking hard and I have an idea. It's something I saw in a film once, a similarly big heist. I think I know how to do it.

At the entrance is a security guard. I say to him, "Excuse me, could I try your uniform on?"

He stares at me then replies, "You need to go to the information desk. It's on the right."

This is a bit weird, but I go there and say to the lady, "Excuse me, I just asked the security guard if I could try his uniform on and he said I should ask here." I accompany this with a look intending to communicate, "How weird is that! That he told me to ask you!" Because this is the weird bit. Not the trying-on-the-uniform bit.

She is very confused. Flummoxed, even. "Well, I mean . . . I've actually no idea. He told you to come here?"

"Yeah," I say. "I thought it was a bit weird."

"I'd imagine it was up to individuals if they let you try their uniform on. I'll check with my colleague."

She leans over to the man next to her. I can tell she is embarrassed by the words coming out of her mouth.

"This lady wanted to try on the security guard's uniform and he sent her over here."

He looks at me incredulously. I match his incredulous look and add, "I know! Why did he send me here?"

He suggests I go back to the security guard. Although he's not sure it would be a good idea for other people to dress up as security guards.

I worry now that I've become too noticeable and am on the

verge of abandoning this amazing plan. But I do return to the security guard and explain that they've sent me back to him.

He looks at me coldly. Then asks with equal coldness, "You want me to take my clothes off?"

"Yes," I say confidently. Even though I'm starting to see small cracks in my plan.

"You'll have to get a job here if you want to wear the uniform," he tells me.

I'll have to find another way to steal the Elgin Marbles.

I go through the museum to the marbles. I realise that I've never seen them in the flesh before. I'm thinking now I'm not sure how much they're actually worth. They are not in a great state. They're also a bit bigger than I thought. They are definitely not going to fit in my canvas bag.

I formulate a new plan. I see two members of staff patrolling the hall. I walk towards them and say, "Hi, Michael and Tom, is it?"

I could be lucky. I'm not.

"No, neither of us, I'm afraid."

"Oh, they must've given me the wrong names. Sorry, I've been sent to take the horse's head from the marbles for cleaning. Could you both give me a hand carrying it out to my taxi?"

It's a no. I'd need to be here with someone with ID. It's very frustrating. I need help. I sidle up to a strong-looking man and say under my breath, "Do you want to help me steal the Elgin Marbles?"

He looks at me and laughs. "What? You're going to give them back to Greece?" he asks as if he's made the greatest joke in the world.

"Yes," I say.

I've got no option but to revert to plan A. If I can find a buyer willing to pay big money, I'm sure the British Museum won't say no. I see someone who looks like a Japanese businessman. I sidle up to him. "Want to buy the Elgin Marbles?"

He runs away from me, literally. He actually runs away and leaves the room.

It's last-resort time. I've got some Post-it notes in my bag. I write on one: *FOR SALE THE ELGIN MARBLES. Contact me* and then my email address.

I stick it up on the wall next to an Elgin Marble. Then leave very quickly. I keep checking my email and there's nothing yet, but maybe there's a problem with money being tied up. Some rich business person is probably selling some portfolios to free up some cash right now.

Later that day I get a voicemail from the British Museum. I'm terrified it's to tell me I'm banned for life. Then I remember the state of the Elgin Marbles and care a little less. But it's from the director of development, in regards to my enquiries yesterday about brokering a deal for the sale of the marbles. She wants me to call back. Despite all evidence to the contrary, including those legal documents, perhaps they will sell them.

I don't want to mess everything up at this late stage though, so it's time for me to pass everything I've learned on to the economic experts. They can take it from here. By which I mean, do the actual deal with the British Museum and then abolish all currency and set up a barter system. But, presuming they won't be impressed by my home economics GCSE, how can I persuade them to listen to me? Then it comes to me. Like a bolt out of the blue. The answer. I'll lie! I'll say I've been studying economics for forty years. I've devoted my life to it. My name is Professor Angela Cleveland.

I try the Treasury first. There's a message saying nobody is available to take my call.

Next up is the World Bank. It's a recorded message telling me to press one for an operator or if calling from a rotary phone, please hold. I'm glad to hear that so many people are calling the World Bank from a rotary phone. I thought the only person still using a rotary phone was Noel Edmonds on *Deal or No Deal* and, presumably, the banker.

I press one for the operator and tell her it's Professor Angela Cleveland calling for the president, Robert Zoellick.

"And what's the nature of the call? Is it regarding a meeting?"

"No, it's a conference call." I've heard business people talk about conference calls before.

"He'll know who you are, then?"

"Oh yes."

"And what school are you from?"

I say with confidence, "Oh, Oxford University."

Professor Angela Cleveland has just got herself a new job.

"Okay, hold there a moment."

I'm waiting for a bit. Then I hear, "Professor Cleveland?" It takes me a while to realise that's me.

The woman tells me that Robert is with a few people at the moment and can he call me back? Of course he can. The president! Of the World Bank! I leave my mobile number.

I try the White House now. The only number I could find was a comments line. I tell the lady who answers that I have a message for Barack Obama. I'm sure she doesn't hear that all the time, followed by something crazy.

I keep it short. "It's Professor Angela Cleveland. I've studied the world economy for forty years. This is how to save the economy. Persuade Britain to sell the Elgin Marbles. Give money to Greece and then abolish all currency and set up a barter system."

She repeats this as she writes it down.

"He'll get to see that?" I ask.

"Yes, it'll go to him at the end of the day," she assures me.

"Really?"

I'm imagining him in an armchair with a whisky, while this lady I'm talking to perches on the arm and reads out his messages.

"Well, his team, really," she says.

This is disappointing but at least someone will see it. I tell her to be sure to mention I've been studying the world economy for forty years.

She replies with, "Well, yes, you sound like you know what you're talking about, so that's great."

This is now my only hope. Barack Obama.

Until 4.45 p.m., when my mobile rings. It's a Washington number. I'm so excited as I answer it. And I'm right to be. It's the chief of staff at the World Bank ringing on behalf of Robert Zoellick as he's tied up in a meeting.

The chief of staff at the World Bank in Washington DC! Calling me! An idiot!

"I wanted to call you back as actually I studied at Oxford," she says. "Which college are you at?"

"Oh," I say, my brain desperately scrambling around for one. "Jesus College."

I then change the subject immediately so we don't get into any Oxford University chat. As while I did go to Oxford Brookes University, I'm not sure my knowledge of the pubs on the Cowley Road is going to help me.

I launch into my suggestions. Starting with the Elgin Marbles and ending with the barter system.

"Okay," she says. Then there's a long pause. It's very possible she's regretting calling me.

"What I think I'll do—" she says then stops again. "The Elgin Marbles – how far along are you with the British Museum?"

"It's early days," I say. "Lots of legal red tape to get through."

"And the barter system – have you been in touch with anyone else?"

"Well, yes, the Treasury here," I tell her, but leave out the bit where, when I got in touch, it went straight to a recorded message.

"Gosh," she says. "Well, we're not directly involved in Greece. We mostly deal with developing countries. What I'll do is mention it to Bob."

Bob! She calls the president Bob!

"Then check if anyone on the economic desk is working on Greece. And then regarding the Elgin Marbles, we'll see if we can help provide any traction on that."

She then asks for my email address so we can touch base later. Obviously I don't have an Oxford University email address so I have very grave concerns that the one I do give her is not entirely convincing.

"It's profangecleveland@gmail.com."

I don't expect to hear from her.

And I'm right.

4

The Challenge:
To achieve immortality

"Annabel, your challenge this week is to become immortal. To live for ever." Sometimes I worry that Geoff sets me up for failure. However, I am very excited about the prospect of immortality. I think it's really embarrassing that trees are living to 3,000 years and yet, at best, we can't make past 120. Trees! It's so embarrassing.

Like so many things, though, it's an area I know little about. I have heard of cryopreservation, where you're frozen after death and then resurrected once they've worked out how. But the only people I know that have signed up are Walt Disney and Simon Cowell. And I'm not keen on the idea that in two hundred years' time there'll be only us three from the past and, like expats, we end up together, in a very weird gang. I suppose I could talk to Simon about *The X Factor* for a bit but then Walt will want to go to Disneyland every weekend and that's going to get tiring. I'm not one for a roller coaster.

But rather than go to the effort of thinking of another option, I start to look into it.

It turns out that Alcor, the biggest cryopreservation company, is based in Arizona. They have already frozen one hundred and six humans and thirty-three pets. Then there's the Cryonics Institute, which has in the deep freeze one hundred and three humans and seventy-six pets. While the new kid on the block is the snappily titled KrioRus with seventeen humans, two cats, four dogs and two birds.

I start looking at the prices of Alcor. A whole body frozen costs $200,000. Just the head is $80,000. I'm really torn now. Just the head is a lot cheaper and I'm really tight. But I can't get rid of the image of just my head on a wheelchair being pushed around by Simon Cowell. And Walt Disney being really happy we can go to the front of the queue for Thunder Mountain.

There's a UK branch of Alcor. To join the mailing list, you are encouraged to go to alcor-uk-subscribe@yahoogroups. com.

There's a nagging voice in my head saying that if I'm going to be spending $200,000 I'd be happier if they had something a little bit more official than a Yahoo! group.

I decide instead to dial the telephone number. It goes to voicemail. Not an Alcor UK voicemail, just the standard one that came with their phone. I leave a message about how I'm looking to be preserved after death. Nobody calls me back.

I reassure myself that these are scientists. They are making brilliant discoveries; you can't expect them to be great at admin as well. And it's not the end of the road. On their webpage, there's also a number for an insurance company because, as they say, most people pay by life insurance.

I call the number. It's out of service. I'm a little reluctant to try the mobile number given, picturing some man in a bedsit, picking up calls while watching *This Morning*. But I'm soon speaking to Graham. I strain to hear Phillip and Holly in the background, but it's silent. We have a long chat and I learn it could be as little as £15 a month for a policy plus the membership fee.

I do the maths. I'm looking at £44 a month. If I die tomorrow, this is really cheap. A total bargain. But if I die at the average age of eighty-two, it's just over £24,000.

This is cheaper than I imagined, but I'm sure I could get it even cheaper. Why can't I just arrange the whole cryopreservation myself? Why not?

The first thing I'd need is a big tank of liquid nitrogen. I look online and find a fifty-litre one for about £600. I'll probably need three of these.

Now all I need is a chest freezer big enough to hold my body. I ring up the Currys' call centre. A woman answers.

"Hello, I'm looking for a chest freezer big enough for a body," I say brightly.

"For a what, sorry?" she replies.

"A body," I say loudly and clearly.

"I'll have a look. We do a lot of chest freezers, I believe."

After a short time, she's back. "Okay, the biggest we have is 175 litres so it would depend on the body size."

I'm stunned by her reaction. She is totally unfazed by my request for a freezer that will hold A BODY. She's almost bored by it all. She needs to know the body size, though, so I tell her.

"It'd be five foot four."

She asks me if the body will be standing.

"No, lying down," I tell her.

"Well, the one I'm looking at here is tall and thin so wouldn't be beneficial to yourself. What price are you thinking?"

"I'm happy to pay any price as long as it fits the body," I say. I emphasise "the body" in case she hasn't yet really processed this part of the request.

There's a short pause. She's found one. It's £350. She gives me the dimensions. It's in centimetres so I tell her I'll convert to inches and then see if it will fit the body. Once again I emphasise "the body".

"Okay," she says and gives me the product code so that I can see it on the website. I take a look. I think it will fit if my knees are a bit bent. I add on the price of the liquid nitrogen and I've got a total of £2,156. DIY cryopreservation for just over two grand.

I'm very happy with this. Although vaguely concerned about who I can trust to keep the freezer plugged in for the next thousand years or so. A giant tortoise? Doctor Who? A tree? I look into one more option as a backup plan and discover another way of living for ever called metempsychosis, where your mind jumps into another body. That way you don't have to be tied down to your own ageing body. You just keep moving round until the end of time.

This is perfect! It's less sciencey than the cryopreservation, so my brain, which only managed a D in GCSE chemistry, might be able to handle it. I just need to learn how to do it.

I find an article on the Internet and press a button that downloads a PDF. A PDF of 313 pages. Scrolling down, I lose the will to live in my own body, let alone anybody else's. But I finally get to the relevant bits.

The first step is to learn to regard your body as a garment.

I try this and find that I immediately want to take my body back for an exchange or refund.

But it says you have to change the way you think about your body. You can't say, "I'm tired," you have to say, "My body is tired." I get a chance to use this straight away and change my thought of, "This is ridiculous," to, "My body thinks this is ridiculous."

It goes on to say you have to really believe in it to work. I try really hard. I remind myself I was once regressed to a past life where I was a milkmaid in Hornchurch and I believed that, so I must be able to do this.

I'm totally ready to learn how to actually do this. I scroll down and realise that was it. There is nothing more. Three hundred and thirteen pages and they've not actually told me how to do it.

I find another piece. This one urges you to ask permission first. I start worrying now. I hadn't really thought it all through. About how there's going to be two of us in this body. Just one voice in my head is exhausting. Two would be horrifying.

And there's still nothing on exactly how to do it. I have read that advanced yogis do it, though. And luckily there's a yoga centre nearby. I go down there and greet the two girls on reception with, "Hi. I'm here for metempsychosis."

They don't know what that is. I explain. They tell me they don't do it. I overreact a bit to this news.

"No! You don't do it? Oh my God! None of your yogis do it?"

They tell me that perhaps they do in their spare time. They do seem very interested in it all. They're asking me a lot of questions. I suddenly feel like I'm the expert, having read two

Internet articles, so I get carried away and find myself saying, "Do you want me to do it on you now?"

They both give a very firm no. They don't. They laugh it off. One says, "I'd be too worried about it. What if I got stuck in a mad woman's body for ever?"

I don't like the way she looks at me when she says "mad woman". I leave in search of a willing participant; it might turn out I'm a natural. It might turn out that, unlike tennis, baking and hula-hooping, I've got an innate special ability. This could be it. The one thing I'm naturally good at. I'm giddy with optimism, when I spot a man standing outside a shop smoking. He's got a large bag by his feet.

I find myself approaching him and saying,

"Excuse me, can I do metempychosis on you? Leave my body and then enter yours."

I wonder if a pervert has ever said this. It sounds a bit like what a pervert might say.

He stares at me then says, "That is the weirdest thing anybody has ever said to me."

I'm relieved he said "weirdest" and not "most perverted". And it's not a no. "Well, do you want to do it?" I say.

If there's one thing I know, and it really is the one thing I know, when it comes to metempychosis you have to ask permission first. He is confused, but some inherent politeness has emerged from him and he's saying yes.

I find myself standing a foot away from a man, facing his side, eyes closed and really trying to leave my own body and enter his.

I start with deep breathing. Occasionally I open my eyes a fraction to check he's still there. He is. Just looking forward. I notice after a bit he's not even smoking any more. Just waiting patiently. Or he might be trying really hard to pretend this is not happening. While I'm trying really hard to spiritually enter his body. This might be the strangest thing I've ever done. After five minutes I stop. I open my eyes. I have to confess to him,

"I'm really sorry. I just couldn't do it. Just as I was about to leave my body something was holding me back."

He looks bewildered, so rather than prolong our interaction, I thank him and leave.

I don't manage to attain immortality by metempsychosis. But I do feel like the cryopreservation is pretty much sorted. All I need to do is find someone to make sure that freezer is kept plugged in for a thousand years or so and then mentally prepare myself for the Port, Cowell and Disney gang.

5

The Challenge: To help the
Occupy protesters

St Paul's Cathedral has looked like a camping site for weeks. The Occupy movement has been protesting against social and economic inequality. There have been similar occupations all over the world, starting in New York on Wall Street. They are continually being moved on and it looks like the St Paul's protesters are next. They need a new space to occupy and it's my job to find it.

I'm concerned. When I wake up it's raining. The last time I went camping I got trench foot, making me perhaps the first person since the First World War to suffer from this. I make my first decision. Wherever the new occupation is, it will be indoors. All I need is my sleeping bag.

The Occupy protesters want to make a big impact, so I need a really big iconic London institution to house them. But my priorities include not just shelter but preferably also access to a bed, food, drink and a bathroom. It seems to me that a good place to occupy would be a hotel. A really big, iconic London hotel. It has to be the Ritz. I've never been there, but I'm sure there's a restaurant. I can go in, sit down and then just not leave.

I arrive at the imposing building. To give you the complete picture, I'm wearing a checked shirt, jeans, trainers and a parka. I'm carrying a handbag and sleeping bag. I'm wondering if I'm the first person ever to carry a sleeping bag into the Ritz.

I go through the revolving doors into a very grand lobby, where a tall man in fancy clothes asks if he can help me. He probably wants to help me find the exit.

"Yes," I say. "I want something to eat."

"Something to eat," he repeats, like nobody has ever come in and said that before.

"Yes," I tell him.

"I'm afraid it's formal wear only in our restaurant."

"What, like ballgowns?" I ask.

"Yes," he says.

I give him a look intending to convey, *Oh I knew I should've worn my ballgown this afternoon.* Meanwhile I'm thinking, *I can't see anyone else in ballgowns, what with it being midday.*

"You could go into the bar where they have snacks, but trainers aren't allowed," he says, looking at my feet.

"Oh, don't worry about that," I tell him. "I'll take them off."

I quickly slip them off and put them in my bag. I'm now just in my socks.

"Have you got other shoes?" he asks.

"Oh yes," I say. This is not a lie. I do have other shoes. Just not with me.

I can tell he's not entirely sure about all this but he directs me to the bar.

Once I'm there, I'm faced with another man. He's wearing a white evening jacket. He greets me with, "How can I help you?" and glances down at my shoeless feet.

"Table for one, please," I say brightly.

He takes me to a table. There are only three others in the bar. They all look like businessmen and they are all wearing shoes. It's a beautiful, grand, art deco-styled room.

It's time to occupy it. I pull my sleeping bag out of its cover and climb in. By the time the man in the white evening jacket has returned with the menu, I am fully inside with my sleeping bag pulled right up to my chest.

The man does not say a word. He just lays the menu before me. I don't look at it. I think that if you have a drink and light snack it counts less as an occupation and more of a lunch. Regardless of the sleeping bag. Eventually he returns to take my order.

"I don't think I'm going to have anything. I think I'm just going to sit here."

"Okay," he says and takes the menu away.

I suddenly realise that the one thing worse than being dragged out of this hotel in a sleeping bag is being ignored and having to sit here for hours until I'm forced to say, "Actually I think I'll go now," to avoid spending the rest of my life in the bar in the Ritz.

I'm sitting there for five long minutes. Then a second barman comes over. He asks me what I'd like to order. I tell him that I'm just having a sit-down.

He's not such a pushover. He tells me I have to consume something or leave, but he'll get me a chair in the gallery.

I don't fancy the sound of this. I could be on a chair in the gallery for a very long time. Until I'm dusty.

I beckon him closer and say conspiratorially, "Do you want to know a secret?"

I can tell from his face that he doesn't want to know any kind of secret from a person in a sleeping bag in the bar of the Ritz, but I plough on regardless.

"I'm occupying the bar like those people at St Paul's."

"Okay," he says smoothly. "Well, in that case I'm going to have to call security, madam."

I wait, secretly pleased that despite the circumstances I am still a "madam". In a short while, a big, friendly-looking man in a suit sits down opposite me. He tells me he's head of security.

"What are you up to?" he asks.

I tell him I'm finding a new home for the Occupy protesters and preferably in more salubrious surroundings.

He explains that this is private property, so I'll have to leave.

"Oh," I say. "Is this like when the Occupy protesters were moved on from Paternoster Square?"

"Well, this is private property," he tells me again.

"Okay," I say. "I'll just pack my sleeping bag away."

I'm suddenly filled with horror. It can take me upwards of five days to pack a sleeping bag back in its cover. It seems to grow the moment it's taken out. It involves me using up a lot of floor space and a lot of puffing air out of both the bag and me. I hadn't considered this. I express my concerns.

"Just stuff it in," he tells me.

It takes ages but we have a lovely chat. About Thailand, east London and his ex-wife.

When I'm finished, I say, "Will you now escort me to the door?"

"Oh yes," he replies, like I'm their oldest customer and nothing is too much trouble. We get to the door, shake hands and I go off on my way.

My advice to St Paul's is: send this man down there to ask them all nicely to leave. They probably will.

I've achieved a lot so far. I've confirmed that the Ritz Hotel is not a suitable place for the Occupy movement to go to next. I just need to find somewhere else.

I definitely want something similar to St Paul's. An iconic institution, a symbol of the Blitz spirit, a big tourist attraction. And it comes to me. The flagship Topshop store at Oxford Circus. It's perfect. And it'll be fun to try on all the clothes when everyone's gone home at night.

I gather up my sleeping bag again. It strikes me that a lot of protesters are wearing masks. I've not got a proper mask at home. But I do have an eye mask so I pack that too.

When I arrive at Topshop, I go down the escalators to the main shopping area and start scouting out a good place to occupy. I find that I'm drawn to corners, but then tell myself it's not much of a protest if you're hiding.

At the bottom of the escalator, right in the middle of the store, are four mannequins. I go in front of them and get out my sleeping bag and eye mask. Once I'm in my sleeping bag, I try putting the mask on, but it's incredibly disconcerting being in the middle of one of London's busiest shops in a sleeping bag and not being able to see. So I wear it on my forehead.

People are staring at me. I feel really, really embarrassed. Perhaps it would be better to cover my eyes.

The staff are milling about but none are trying to move me on. I notice a security guard look at me and then look away again very quickly. I think he's pretending he hasn't seen me as he doesn't want to have to deal with a person on the shop floor in a sleeping bag.

After about ten minutes, another security guard, who I'd describe as beefy, approaches me and says, "I'm going to have to ask you to leave."

I explain what I'm doing and he walks off without a word.

I start to get nervous. What if he's calling police? I don't want a criminal record. What if I get through to judges' houses in *The X Factor* next year but Simon Cowell is the mentor and I can't get a visa to go to his house in Los Angeles. These are very real concerns.

Some more people have arrived. They're not police, but they are plain-clothed security. And they are not friendly.

They tell me it's private property and one of the men adds, "You've made your point, you've got lots of publicity at St Paul's. You don't need to be here."

I realise that he thinks I'm actually one of the Occupy London group. I have very mixed feelings. I admire the dedication of these protesters, but the parka I'm wearing is actually from Selfridges. Can't they tell?

He then says, "I'm going to ask you once more to leave." The unspoken threat hangs in the air.

I climb out of my sleeping bag. Surprisingly, the two men start packing it away for me in its cover, but they're really rubbish at it. They give up and tell me to do it myself outside. I just start stuffing it in, adding that I was advised to do it this way by someone at the Ritz.

The least friendly one escorts me up the escalators. As

we're going up I say, "I'm not banned, am I? It's just that I get a lot of my clothes from here."

"What?" he says.

"Yes, this shirt I'm wearing is from here."

He gives me an incredulous look mixed in with quite a lot of disgust. We get to the door and he turns to face me and says the following: "You are on camera here. I am now verbally banning you from this store. If you ever attempt to re-enter you will be trespassing and the police will be called."

I burst out laughing. "You don't think this is a bit of an overreaction do you?"

He doesn't share my sense of humour.

I leave. I'm gutted. I get nearly all my clothes in Topshop. I can only go back to my favourite shop in disguise. This is terrible.

Maybe Topshop was a bad idea. And one thing that's bothered me about the whole St Paul's occupation is why are these church people being inconvenienced? It's the inequalities of the global financial system that the occupiers are protesting against.

I should occupy a bank and I know exactly which bank. The poshest one. Coutts. The Queen's own bank.

I'm also starting to think that it's no good testing a place on my own. There are over 200 tents at St Paul's. I need to get others to join me.

I try asking outside Coutts. I approach a young man first.

"I'm just going to go and occupy Coutts like they've done at St Paul's, will you do it with me?"

"Do you know what, I've got an appointment. I'm so sorry."

I ask a lady. As soon as the words are out of my mouth I realise my mistake. She looks like Natasha Kaplinsky. She is never going to join me in my sleeping bag. I try lots of people, but nobody wants to come with me.

I go in on my own. It's very posh. There's wood panelling, an elaborate ceiling with lots of little gold lion heads on it and the glass panels that separate you from the three cashiers go all the way up to the high ceiling.

One man is being served. He looks and sounds posh. I see a small armchair so take a seat.

One of the cashiers asks me, "Are you okay there?"

I wave and say, "Hi."

The man being served is now walking around a bit while the lady is doing something.

I try and attract his attention with a, "Psst!"

He either doesn't hear or he is ignoring me.

I do it again. "Psst!"

He looks over.

I say in a loud stage whisper, "I'm occupying the building, do you want to join me?"

He smiles politely and mouths the words, "No thank you."

He finishes his business and leaves.

The woman who had been serving him now says to me, "Are you okay there? Can I help you?"

"No, I'm just occupying."

She starts to do the polite and smiling, "Right, okay," and then registers what I'm saying and stops.

"Like at St Paul's," I add.

She immediately goes somewhere behind the scenes. She's gone a while. The other two cashiers are staring at me. I give them a big smile.

One starts asking questions. She's very friendly.

"Are there others coming?"

"Not at the moment."

"Are you doing this on your own?"

"Yes."

"How long are you going to be here for?"

"I don't know."

Then the first lady returns and makes a phone call. I can't hear what she is saying but soon the world's oldest security man appears. He shuffles through a door and over to a water cooler. He gets a drink of water and then just shuffles around the lobby.

I smile at him and say, "Hello."

He says hello back. But nothing else. He keeps looking out of the door and I'm very nervous he's called the police.

"Would you like me to leave?" I say to him.

"Well, yes. That would be nice," he replies gratefully.

"I'm going to do whatever you say," I tell him.

"Well, if you wouldn't mind," he says.

I say goodbye to the cashiers. They seem really surprised I'm going and, if I'm not mistaken, disappointed. I get the distinct impression they would've liked me to stay longer.

So, in a way I've found the perfect place, but the security guard was so nice that I wouldn't want him to have any unnecessary stress. I can only conclude that the best place for these protesters, based on my extensive research, would be Topshop. I suspect the ban for life won't bother them too much. And I've made my big sacrifice for social and economic justice. As I can now only shop there online.

6

The Challenge: To do something
no woman has done before

This challenge begins with me wasting a good chunk of time
fantasising about being mentioned in the same breath as
fellow female trailblazers Edith Wharton (first female Pulitzer
Prize for Fiction winner), Amelia Earhart (first female to
fly the Atlantic solo), Valentina Tereshkova (first woman
in space), Elizabeth Blackwell (first female doctor), Marie
Curie (first female Nobel Prize winner), Benazir Bhutto (first
female leader of a Muslim state), Sirimavo Bandaranaike
(first female head of government) and Kathryn Bigelow (first
female director to win an Oscar).

Which is going to require a really long breath. I spend
some time testing whether it's even possible. It is, just about.

My procrastination comes from confidence. There must be
loads of different things women have never done. I go on the
Internet. And immediately panic. There is no complete list of
all the things women haven't done yet. It's very hard to find

any. I'm googling "things a female has never done" and the only result is a thread on a bodybuilding website forum where a man has posted "a female has never made me laugh".

I briefly consider attempting it, but it would mean having contact with this despicable man.

I start thinking of all the obvious ones.

I know for sure there's never been a female president of the USA. The only thing holding me back right now is that they're not advertising for a new president. Plus, I wasn't born in the USA. And I know nothing about politics.

First female pope is my next thought. But once again, they're not currently advertising for a new pope. And I'm not Catholic. Or religious. Besides, there might have already been a female Pope. Pope Joan, if the legend is to be believed. And to be Pope, she had to pretend to be a man until she blew it by giving birth during a procession and I don't fancy doing either of those things.

I should perhaps scale down my ambition. Then I think, what about the moon? No woman has ever been on the moon. But realistically, is this achievable? Ever the optimist, I look into it.

It's not great news. You need a degree in engineering, bio-logical science, physical science or mathematics. I fulfil one element of this. In that I've got a degree. And is English litera-ture so different from physical science? I don't know. As I'm not entirely sure what physical science is.

A science degree is not enough for these space types though. Oh no. They also require that you have 1,000 flying miles as a pilot-in-command. But there is some good news. I am tall enough. You must be between sixty-two and seventy-three inches and I'm sixty-three inches. I'm so pleased and excited about this I briefly forget the degree and the 1,000 flying miles. And that there are no plans to put anyone at the moon at the moment.

That's fine, though. I don't really want to go to the moon. There's nothing there and that spacesuit is not at all flattering. I'd look fat and like I've got a big head.

I move on. Other female firsts yet to happen are dictator, White House chief of staff, UN secretary general, director of a Bond movie and Dalai Lama, which I quite fancy as they wear very autumnal colours and that's my season, colour-wise.

Then I realise that while there has been a female Beefeater at the Tower of London, there's not yet been a female Beefeater Ravenmaster. This could be interesting. And in terms of a job, surely loads easier than being the American president. It probably just means feeding the ravens. And as long as they don't eat really fancy cooked meals, that'll be fine.

I look it up. It turns out they're fed raw meat, which puts me off a bit as I've not eaten meat for over twenty years. But I could shake things up a bit and give them raw Quorn. Who are the ravens going to tell? Although it would be bad if they left the Tower to find meat, as then the monarchy would fall. And while for many anti-royalists this would be a good thing, I wouldn't want to be responsible for the Queen living on the streets.

I realise I'm getting distracted again and continue with my research. It's good to know your enemy, and the current Ravenmaster is my enemy. I find out his name is Chris. I feel like I know enough now and move on. I discover that to become a Beefeater you have to be retired from the armed forces. I'm briefly worried, then remember I've been paint-balling twice so that should be enough. It's the same thing. Ish.

I'm thinking I'll turn up, say I'm the new Ravenmaster, Chris gets his coat, I get out the Quorn or tofu and get to work.

Then I do something unusual for me. I have a bit more of a think. I'm now wondering, maybe the thing to do is show up and say I'm the new assistant Ravenmaster. That way, Chris doesn't lose his job and I still get to do a first – first-ever female assistant Ravenmaster. As well as the first-ever assistant Ravenmaster. A double first!

I google a bit more and find out who top dog is at the Tower. It's Colonel Richard Harrold. Then I head off to claim my place in history.

I start off at the Welcome Centre. I'm sure Edith Wharton, Amelia Earhart and Benazir Bhutto began their journey into the history books at a Welcome Centre too.

There's a lady at the desk. I give her a big smile.

"Hi! I'm here to see Chris. I'm the new assistant Raven-master."

She tells me I need to go to the pass office. There is no sign of any surprise on her face.

I go to the pass office. I tell the man there I'm here to see Chris as I'm the new assistant Ravenmaster.

"Assistant Ravenmaster," he repeats. Then mutters to himself, "Well, he didn't tell me about this."

He's rummaging around the paperwork on this desk. Perhaps hoping to find a memo from Chris about this new position.

He then picks up the phone and makes a call asking to speak to Chris. It seems someone is going to find Chris and get him to call back. He hangs up.

"Assistant," he says again.

I confirm this.

"It's usually a Beefeater," he says. Then adds, "You're not a Beefeater, certainly."

I'm a little bit insulted. Why is he so sure? I could be. Before I can say any of this, we're interrupted by the phone ringing.

He picks it up. "Got a young lady here says she's to be the assistant Ravenmaster."

There's a note of disbelief in his voice but I'm so thrilled he called me "young lady" that I don't care.

He doesn't say anything else apart from, "Right, yes, okay," and hangs up.

Here we go! I'm mentally getting ready for the ravens. I'm picturing myself in a Beefeater outfit. I like wearing red. I'm wondering if I dare combine it with a red lipstick when the man says: "Sorry, he doesn't know anything about it and he's not working today."

I'm a bit worried as to who is feeding the ravens today, then. Are they pecking each other's eyes out? But I've got to think of me and my job so I say, "Oh, it's just that Colonel Richard Harrold called me and said I had the job."

As I'm sure this is the kind of thing a colonel does. Make personal phone calls to assistants offering them jobs. I'm sure.

"Dick?" says the man

"Yeah, Dickie," I say.

Somewhat miraculously, he doesn't question this further and says instead, "It's very unusual. Only Beefeaters do this. Are you ex-army?"

This is the most ridiculous question I've ever been asked. I've clearly never been on an assault course in my life. My arms look like they'd snap if I tried to do a press-up. I do own a nice camo-print dress though and consider telling him about it. Then decide against it.

"No," I tell him. "But I've been paintballing twice."

He laughs. It's a bit of a weary laugh. I didn't add that I hated paintballing and that the second time I went I walked off after five minutes to sit in the car.

"Sorry I can't help you," he says.

He's a nice man so I don't want to pester him. But I am worried about who is feeding the ravens today. I ask him.

He assures me someone else will be doing it. I ask if I can help them. It's a no.

I leave. And it's fine. I don't even like ravens. And ravens probably don't like Quorn. And actually, I think I have achieved a female first. I think I probably am the first woman to ever try and blag her way into a job as the assistant Raven-master at the Tower of London.

7

The Challenge:
To become a prepper

I'd never heard of preppers, this community of people preparing for Doomsday. I didn't know I had to prepare for civilisation breaking down. I just assumed I'd be scrabbling around in the dirt in raggedy clothes. I didn't know there was an alternative.

My only experience of this kind of thing was about eight years ago when my mum came up to London with a disaster-survival kit for me, which from memory was eight litres of water and eight tins of Waitrose ratatouille. All were gone within a year and she never replenished it as her first grand-child, my niece, was born not long after and I've since been dead to her.

I don't feel I would survive very long in any kind of end-of-the-world situation. I can't light a fire and I'm a very fussy eater so would probably starve from lack of tomatoes and penne pasta. I was never in the Girl Guides so didn't learn anything there. I'm not even sure I want to live in a world without the Internet. I've clearly got some work to do.

I go online and read about a man from Phoenix who has 1,000 tilapia fish in his swimming pool, to provide food for him when a massive solar flare ends the world as we know it. There's a couple with 25,000 rounds of ammunition and enough food to keep them going for fifty years. Another woman regularly practises fleeing the city by foot as she's convinced there will be an oil crisis. Another couple spend fifty hours a week preparing for the drastic effects of a climate shift in the poles.

Fifty hours a week is a full-time job. I find myself thinking that there is a good chance they are wasting their lives. Then I remember what I do for a living and shut up.

This is all in America, though. I want to know what is going on in the UK and I find a big website for British preppers. There's a forum, which is great; I can just join that and get talking to the preppers. I can't find anywhere to register, though, and eventually I see this post: *New users registrations disabled. This is until further notice.*

This was posted on Sunday afternoon, just two days ago, what is going on? Then I see how many members they already have at the bottom of the page and I know why: 1,234 members. The number 1,234 has probably got some special meaning in numerology like, "those that prepare will live".

I'm pretty gutted. I'd already chosen my username of Apocalypse Annabel. Luckily, I can still read the posts. The subject of the most recent one is: *What are you doing to prep this week?* This is a good starting point for me. The most recent response is:

> I've bought six boxes of paracetamol, four tubes of
> toothpaste, 2 x 20m of catering foil, 2 x 20m cling film
> and 4kg of sugar.

I'm really struggling to see how this is going to help when the end is nigh. It's nice they'll be able to wrap lots of stuff. But twenty metres of cling film would be no good to me; I'd have completely lost the end of it about ten centimetres in.

I look for other posts and see this one:

> Took delivery of an online shopping order today and
> the delivery man said he had never delivered such a
> large order even though he delivers to businesses and
> nurseries. So I lied and said it was a joint order between
> me and a friend.
>
> I've managed to cart it all upstairs and put half of it
> away, but have given up now to have brew and go and
> walk the dogs.
>
> Oh yes, and the 270 loo rolls arrived last week.
> Delivery man thought he was delivering a fridge-freezer,
> the box was that big.

Someone then asks him where he keeps it all:

> The loo roll is in the alcove behind my bed.
> I have several boxes of stuff under the bed.
> I have a chest of drawers which is full of tins of fruit
> and veg.
>
> Underneath it I have twenty five-litre bottles of water.
> And a bottle of Vimto.

He'll be glad of that Vimto, when he's surrounded by the decomposing, starved bodies of the non-preppers. And even gladder of his clean bottom.

It's very frustrating not being able to join the forum so I find another big UK preppers site that is accepting new members. I go to register. Unusually for me, I first have a quick look at the terms and conditions and see this:

If you are a Journalist/Reporter/Media Investigator then you are **prohibited** from registering with these forums without **PRIOR** written permission from Dark Vengeance (Site Owner).

I am terrified of Dark Vengeance. I was already scared about how much toilet roll I've got to buy and store, and now someone called Dark Vengeance is threatening me.

I take a deep breath, ignore it, and click on accept. I'm really pleased that I get to use my user name, Apocalypse Annabel. I activate my account and then I get a message. It's from Dark Vengeance.

I'm horrified. Until I see it's an automatic message. I have to post an introduction, which will be invisible until Dark Vengeance has read it and then I have full access. It'd be easier for me to join the Freemasons.

I post my introduction:

I'm a new member. I've decided to stop being a sucker and start preparing for the end of the world as we know it. I don't want to be one of these people, starving and in rags, trying to break into the house of a prepper. I want to be barricading my front door holding a shotgun while looking lovingly at my stockpiled baked beans, bottled water and wind-up radios.

So it all starts today. Any advice appreciated.

While I wait to hear back from Dark Vengeance, I take a look at what others have written in their introduction. Turns out it's just a quick hi, where they're from, that kind of thing. I probably should've checked that first.

I also see that the site has an online store where you can buy essentials. This is great; I can get stockpiling. I click on it and it just looks a lot like a list of camping equipment. Tents, compasses, inflatable pillows, pen knives. If the end of the world survival means camping, you can count me out. I am not camping for the rest of my life. I hate camping.

There's also a notebook that you can write on in the rain and a telescopic pen. I'm not sure how these are things you can't survive without. I don't remember in *The Day of the Triffids* someone saying, "It's very sad, but Helen, although she had a lot of camping equipment, tried to write in the rain on normal paper with a normal pen and sadly died."

I don't buy any of things, mainly because I'm more thinking of stockpiling tampons, lip balm, anti-ageing moisturiser, Bendicks Bittermints and coffee. Things I'm genuinely worried about living without.

I move on to the food-storage calculator that tells me what I need for three months. It includes 360 litres of water. This is a lot of water. My skin is going to look great while everyone else perishes around me. It also recommends ninety sanitary towels. That's thirty a month. Are they doubling up as bedding? Or are they assuming I've got an elephant's womb? They also suggest six deodorants. I don't want to sound cruel, but if you are getting through two deodorants a month, maybe it's better if you're dead.

Being a prepper is really expensive. But my bigger concern is about whether Dark Vengeance has found out I'm from the media. I go back to the forum to see if I've been accepted.

I have! An admin called Luddite (good name) says:

> Hi, and welcome, hope you enjoy your time with us.

But then:

> I've edited your intro slightly – there's a time and a place for talk like that, and the intro section isn't it.

I look back and Luddite has only taken out the shotgun bit. And then I notice I have replies welcoming me from all over the country. All in the few hours since my post went live. I feel very welcome. These are now my people. It'll be just me and them soon. I reply with:

> Hi everyone. I'm from London. I'm ready to get started – what shall I do first?

Within ten minutes I get a response:

> read and learn – heaps of excellent info on here ... then assess your own personal situation.

I was hoping for a bit more interaction so I post:

> It says on the product-storage calculator that as a single woman I'd need to make sure I have six deodorants and ninety sanitary towels for three months – this seems like a lot. Do you think this amount is necessary?

The response is:

> hi there hun … always good to have too much than too
> little hope you enjoy the site and a warm welcome from
> the wet and freezing valleys of south wales first thing to
> do is,,,, grab a cuppa, sit back, relax and have a good read
> through the posts on here as there is a huge amount of
> good info on here

There are other similar replies. I'm not 100% sure I want to live in a world populated solely by people with such terrible grammar. But they are lovely to me. I'm still a bit nervous about being killed by Dark Vengeance for being in the media, but then I do some searching on the site and find out his name is actually Alan and I'm fine again.

It's been nice chatting to preppers online but I want to get more in with them. I want to meet them in person. It strikes me that a good place to find them is either at a supermarket doing a giant shop or in some kind of survival-gear shop. As I don't want to pester someone with a weirdly large family or bulimia, I opt for the latter.

I look online and discover there's a shop near Bond Street called the Survival Shop. It's perfect. Until I get there and find it's closed down. It seems to me there's less demand for end-of-the-world stuff than these preppers believe. Or they just overestimated the demand for rainproof notebooks.

I move to plan B. A camping store. It's quite busy. I go up to a man shopping alone.

"Are you ready for the end of the world as we know it?"

"What?" he says. He appears to be American.

"The end of the world, are you ready for it? I'm getting ready for it."

"I don't know what I'm doing in the next two hours, let alone the end of the world."

He's not one of us. So I say to him, "Well, it looks like I'll survive and you'll perish."

"Oh no," he says. "I've got guns in the States. You'll be coming to me."

I tell him I'll see him then but I don't ask for his address.

I move on to another man looking at Pac-a-Macs. I'm sure these could be useful come the apocalypse so I ask him, "Are you getting ready for the end of the world as we know it?"

"Yes!" he replies.

This is great. However, on further questioning it emerges he was getting "preparing for the end of the world as we know it" confused with "preparing for a trip next year".

I move on again. I decide to start asking the staff. This would be a great place to work for a prepper, you must get a good discount on all the stuff.

I go to a staff member and say, "Excuse me, are you preparing for the end of the world as we know it?"

He looks like he was expecting another kind of question. Then tells me that he's not getting ready. There's another member of staff nearby. I say to him, "I was just asking your colleague if you're preparing for the end of the world as we know it."

"No, we're not. Not in this store, no," he says earnestly.

I'm not giving up. But I have got distracted at this point by a compact first-aid kit and a survival bag that "helps prevent body-heat loss". I'm looking at these kinds of products in a new light. In terms of how useful they'd be, come Doomsday.

I'm seriously thinking about getting them when a member of staff approaches me to ask if I want any help.

"Are you a prepper?" I ask him.

"I'm not," he says. "But I know what you're on about."

It turns out he's seen a show called *Doomsday Preppers* on the National Geographic Channel. He's quite enthusiastic about it, so I'm getting the impression he's more of a prepper than he wants to admit. I push him and eventually he concedes that while he's physically not preparing, he is psychologically. He means he's not stockpiling goods, but he's mentally ready for any eventuality, and that's the important thing. He doesn't see the point in having loads of food at home as he'd be on the move anyway. He'd not be staying barricaded in, and having survival skills is more useful than buying loads of stuff.

We have a great chat about all this. Between him and the online preppers, I've learned so much. I just need to go home now and build my own bunker, plan my escape route, grow all my own food, learn to shoot, build a fire, dehydrate some food and ask my mum to send me eight more tins of Waitrose ratatouille.

8

The Challenge:
To sell myself to Google

Geoff has been thinking about start-up companies, like Skype or Spotify, getting valued for vast sums and then sold. It has given him an idea.

"You could try and get bought by Google."

"Me? As a human being?" This is a very rational question that I'm asking.

"Yes, they seem to be buying up a lot of stuff. Start-ups, Motorola, loads of websites."

"Will you buy me back if I'm not happy?"

I don't get a satisfactory answer. He just reiterates that he wants me to get sold to Google for a vastly inflated price.

This challenge doesn't even make any sense. I'm a person, not a company. A person with no discernible skills. I have nothing to add to their business. Why would Google buy me?

But, like how some people dream of going to Antarctica or the moon, I have always wanted to go to the Google offices.

To see for myself the fireman's pole, the ball pool, the room with puppies, the other room that is just filled with bubble wrap, and the roller coaster.

They are near Victoria station, in a building shared with American Express. Google has the third, fourth and fifth floors. I know this because I'm at the main reception. I tell the man at the desk that I'm here for Google. He takes my name and asks for the name of the person that I'm meeting.

"The head of acquisitions," I say, trying to have the look of someone who's about to be bought for millions. I mostly just do this by maintaining eye contact.

"I need a name," he says.

I hadn't even checked if acquisitions is an actual department, let alone the name of the head.

I pretend to check my phone. Then say the first name that comes into my head, David Merchant. He taps at his keyboard, prints me out a visitor pass, then tells me it's the fifth floor. I'm off!

I go up in the lift to the fifth floor. There's another reception. Google is lot more corporate, with its many receptions, than I'd like. It's also very busy. I take a second to have a good look around and I notice there's a door to my right, which appears to lead to a canteen. You need to tap your electronic pass to get in but some people are coming out.

I stride straight though. Straight through into a different world. It's like when those kids went through that wardrobe into Narnia. I'm in the most amazing canteen ever. There's a smoothie bar. A coffee bar, where you can add any coffee flavouring that you could possibly desire. There's food from what seems like every country of the world. Every condiment ever invented is on a table. There are desserts, chocolate bars, a revolving tray deposit, a big sunny balcony. It's incredible. It's only later that I find out it's also all free.

But I'm not here to eat. I go back to reception with its bowler-hat lightshades, lava lamps and jars of chewing gum and Drumstick lollies.

There are three receptionists. By way of comparison, at my work there's one and when she's on her lunch break she's covered by someone on work experience.

I speak to one of the women and tell her I'm here to see the head of acquisitions. I'm told once more that I need a name.

I try David Merchant again, just in case by some miracle it's right. It's not. I pretend to check my emails on my phone again, but actually I'm on Google trying to find a name. All I can come up with is the head of Google UK, Matt Brittin. He'll do. It's probably best to go straight to the top.

"Oh, it's Matt Brittin," I say.

"That's who you're meeting?" There is definitely an element of disbelief in her voice.

"Yes," I say confidently.

"That's who your email is from?" There's still that element of disbelief. If anything, it's getting stronger.

"Yes," I say firmly.

She starts doing some typing. It's possible she's emailing the woman next to her with the words: *Nutter. Please help.*

I pretend to read the non-existent email when really I'm skimming an article about Matt Brittin and learn that he rowed for Cambridge and got bronze at the 1998 World Rowing Championships.

"Ha! He mentions his rowing in the email."

She looks up at me and says, "Do you want to take a seat?"

I sit and wait. Eventually she calls me over and tells me that I'm wrong, I don't have a meeting with Matt Brittin.

"That's weird," I say looking very puzzled. "Because, you know, the email."

"What email address was it from?" she asks.

"Matt dot Brittin."

"And the rest of it?" There's a challenging tone in her voice.

"At Gmail dot com."

"No. That's not it." I can tell that she's thrilled.

"How weird," I say. I'm not really sure what to do now. So I ask, "While I'm here can I go in the ball pool?"

I'm embarrassed to be saying it. But I have very little dignity left to lose.

"The what?" she says.

I'm forced to repeat myself. "The ball pool."

"We don't do tours of the building."

She's admitted they have a ball pool!

"You have a ball pool!" I say.

"No, we don't," she replies.

She's denying they have a ball pool.

This is not going well. I ask to take a Drumstick lolly and also one for my friend and then go to leave.

As I'm getting back in the lift, ringing in my ears are her words, "We don't do tours of the building."

I take the lift down from the fifth floor, and as the doors open on the fourth to let more people in, a bad voice in my head says, "Oh, don't you now." I get out of the lift. I follow some others through the doors they've opened with a pass and I'm in. Nobody is stopping me. I'm on the loose in Google HQ.

The first thing I notice are the many cafes. Every corner I

turn has a cafe. I see a breakfast bar with every different kind of cereal. How can that all-you-can-eat 10-star buffet not be enough?

There's an area flooded with light and carpet that looks like grass. It has deckchairs dotted about and people are hanging out, chatting and doing a bit of work.

There's an area with whiteboards and beanbags. I see people chatting on phones in proper old red telephone boxes. There are work pods, blackboards, mobile-phone charging pods.

It's amazing. But I don't see a fireman's pole or any puppies, and I don't trip over remote-control robots running messages everywhere.

My fear of being caught is now stronger than my desire to find the ball pool. I'm nervous about being arrested for industrial espionage. As that will really blow my chances at being bought. So I leave.

I've not managed to sell myself to Google. But unexpectedly, I do have a big impact on the company. I report back on the radio show that night about my failure and my little unofficial tour of the offices. Then a few days later, it reaches me that somebody high up at Google heard and ordered an urgent security review. Which is really annoying. I had planned to go back to that canteen for breakfast, lunch and dinner for the next ten years.

9

The Challenge: To make London
lovely again after the riots

The world seems like a scary place at the moment. Thousands of people have been rioting in London and other cities in England. Geoff's solution? Me. It's up to me to prove that London is still lovely, starting with my own area.

I recently moved to Snaresbrook. It's not exactly central London, more not quite Essex. It could be called suburbia. The first day I moved in, I got chatting to my neighbours and they mentioned they had some friends staying but they'd "gone into London" for the day. I thought I was in London! I was horrified. I'm very touchy about my new address and will often petulantly point out I have a London 0208 number, even though I've not actually had a landline for years.

A good place to start would be my neighbourhood shops. The rioters have been smashing shop windows, looting and setting things on fire. Instead of this, I could clean them or do odd jobs.

I go to the closest ones on the high street in Wanstead. It's about a ten-minute walk from my house. There's a travel agent, which is unusual to still see open.

I'm expecting to see one old man staffing it. There's not, there's six young people. There's enough work for six people!

I announce to them all, "Hi, I'm an anti-rioter. I'm not here to smash up your business."

They look a bit nervous. They're probably thinking, *Why is she saying this? Is it a double bluff?*

"I know a lot of small businesses have been hit, so I'm here to do the opposite to yours. Would you like your windows cleaned?"

All six stare at me in disbelief. Eventually one of them tells me they've got a cleaner already.

"It's free," I tell them. "And I've brought a non-toxic glass cleaner and some kitchen roll."

They are still declining. They actually look quite freaked out. I glance back at the windows and notice the windowsill is quite dirty.

"Actually, I can't help noticing your windowsill is pretty dirty. No offence."

I pull some lime antibacterial wipes from my bag and give it a very good wipe.

"Why are you doing this?" one of them asks.

"I just wanted to show that not all young people are bad. Some us are doing good."

I mentally dare them to challenge the fact that I'm the young one, when I'm quite clearly in my mid-to-late thirties.

They are looking at me quizzically, but don't say a word.

I go back to my cleaning. When I finish, I don't want to

put the dirty wipe back in my bag so I pass it to the person closest. She takes it.

"Well, if there's nothing else I can do, I'll be off."

They thank me and I leave.

I go to a newsagent. The lady there doesn't want my help but seems happy to be asked. Next is a florist. She is lovely. "Go and help those that need it," she says, and then thanks me profusely.

In an estate agent, the two men are very confused when I tell them that, "I'm an anti-rioter here to help you."

It emerges that they thought I'd said I was an "anti-writer". That'd I'd be going in there with a giant eraser and Tippex, rubbing out all writing. When I offer my cleaning services, they refuse, saying they've got a cleaner, but perk up considerably when I add that it's free.

"Look at those handprints on your window. I'm going to clean those." I get to work. While I'm cleaning the windows of the estate agent with my non-toxic glass cleaner, we have a nice chat about the rioters.

I really feel like I've got to know my local shopkeepers. Although not in the way I'd hoped when I moved in.

I'm ready to move even closer to home. My neighbours. My street is already really friendly so I go to the next street along and start knocking on doors. There's nobody in. I'm starting to worry that I look like an opportunistic burglar. There are dogs barking and it feels like curtains are twitching and the Neighbourhood Watch is grinding into action.

Eventually, a door is opened by a youngish guy in glasses. I greet him with, "Hi, I've just moved into the neighbourhood and thought I'd come and meet everyone."

He replies, "Oh, my mum's not in at the moment."

I'm obviously now visibly of an age where people in their twenties assume I'm there for their mum.

I tell him it doesn't matter and start asking him questions. I discover he's just graduated and moved back home and he's looking for a job and likes Japanese art. It's going well. It's time to test the neighbourly spirit of the area.

"While I'm here, could I borrow half a cup of sugar?"

There's a pause. Presumably filled with him thinking, *Could you not go to a shop?* Then he says, "What kind?"

"Ooh, what do you mean?"

"Well, sugar cubes or . . ."

"Sugar cubes would be perfect."

I'm impressed. I thought only cafes had sugar cubes. I didn't realise people had them at home. This will be much easier for me to transport.

He disappears into the house, leaving the door open. It's very trusting and he's gone ages. I grow concerned that he's calling social services, or lacing the sugar with arsenic or, worse still, he's found he's not got cubes and gone out the back door to buy some.

Eventually he returns with a huge bag of brown sugar cubes. This is wonderful. London feels very lovely. It's mostly just being lovely to me, but I've got sugar cubes to take home and pretend my flat is a cafe, so I'm very happy.

Happy enough that I try another house. This door is opened by a friendly looking man, who is probably in his early sixties. I tell him I'm new to the area and popped by for a chat. I silently pray that he doesn't say he'll just get his mum. His face lights up and immediately calls behind him, "Liz, come here!"

Liz isn't his mum. Liz is his wife and his name is Chris. I'm talking to them both for so long that I seriously think I could now go on *Mastermind* with my specialist subject of Liz and Chris. I learn how long they've lived there, where they were before that, their complete job history, including modes of transport used for each, all about the other neighbours.

I give up knocking on doors now as there's plenty of people on the street. I see a girl about the same age as me.

"I've got a sore shoulder from carrying my bags, could you give it a massage for me?"

She looks horrified and declines with a firm no. Although she does add, "I don't do massage," before she walks off.

There's a man coming out of some flats. He's in his late fifties and he's stocky, bald and wearing sunglasses, a jumper and checked shorts.

I start telling him my problem. About how my shoulder's sore from carrying my bag. Without a word he holds out his hands to take my bag from me to carry.

"Oh no, I was hoping for a shoulder massage," I say, proffering my shoulder.

He's still not said a word as he gets to work on my shoulder. It's a good massage.

"Have you done this before?" I ask.

"Yes, bunny rabbit," he says.

"On a bunny rabbit?"

"No," he says, laughing incredulously. "You're a bunny rabbit."

I tell him that I'm not.

"You don't want to be cute and cuddly?" he asks.

"Well . . ." I start to say.

"You know Johnny Rotten?"

I tell him I do.

"He said all girls were bunny rabbits."

Suddenly I'm not the mental one. He continues massaging my shoulder the whole time. He may be mental but he's really lovely. When it eventually ends, we go our separate ways. Apart from it's the same way. I have to keep behind him and he's walking really slowly. It's all a bit awkward.

I've really got to know my neighbours though. Once again, not in the way I'd hoped to. But I still don't feel like I've properly integrated with any young people yet. Maybe it's because they're all out rioting. Or maybe not. Maybe the vast majority are just lovely. Now is the time to test it.

There's another high street in South Woodford, about ten minutes from my flat. It includes a Sainsbury's, Marks & Spencer and Laura Ashley Home. There's also a cinema. I see a group of young boys outside. They're about fourteen and eating popcorn.

I say, "Hi, young people! Do you want to come and loot Laura Ashley Home Store with me?"

They stare at me open-mouthed. They don't say a word.

"Come on! Let's get curtains!" I urge them.

Eventually one speaks. "Nah."

"Why?" I ask.

"We're going to see a film."

They don't want to go looting. They are far too nice. My only criticism is that they're eating their popcorn before even going in to the cinema, so are clearly unable to resist instant gratification.

I look for more loveliness. I see four young girls outside Greggs the Baker.

"Hi, young people, my self-esteem is really low today. Could you say some nice things to cheer me up?"

Without missing a beat one says, "I really like your scarf." Immediately followed by another girl saying, "Nice coat." Another one tells me I've got a nice bag. The last one looks me up and down and says, "Yeah, good fashion sense."

I'm so happy I nearly cry. I'd asked some young people to comment on my appearance. I was prepared for the worst, but they are so nice. Not once do they give any indication that this was a strange thing to happen. And one girl thinks I've got good fashion sense. And didn't even add "for your age". Which proves that London is definitely, undeniably, lovely once more.

10

The Challenge: To leak some
confidential information

I'm worried. In the first year of WikiLeaks, they leaked 1.2 million documents. That's 137 an hour. How am I going to manage that?

I decide to start in my own workplace, the radio station. Not because I'm too lazy to leave the building, but because someone once left a list of everybody's salary on the printer, so I think it will be easy.

It starts very badly. A search of all printers just turns up a request for "Shiny Happy People" and some two-for-one vouchers for the restaurant Wok To Walk. I'm going to have to think of another way to access all the confidential information in the building.

I consider hacking into someone's computer but I haven't yet mastered Excel, so I might struggle with hacking.

I can do eavesdropping, though. I can eavesdrop on the high-powered meetings. I know from eighties sitcoms that the best way to do this is by using an upturned glass. I find a clean, empty glass, which in itself is a minor miracle in our building, and I worry that I've used up all my luck already.

Then I go to the fourth floor, the sales floor, which is really intimidating. There's a lot of high-fiving and whooping as yet another big-bucks deal has been closed. I imagine. I haven't been up there since 2003. I'm pretty scared. But I tell myself that if Julian Assange had been scared, we wouldn't have found out that Prince Andrew was a bit rude abroad once, and I force myself up the stairs.

Straight away, I see the meeting room with one of the CEOs and a bigwig from finance inside. The reason I'm able to see this is because all the internal walls are made of glass, a fact that I'd inconveniently forgotten. I don't even know if an upturned glass works on glass. But I do know that me standing with my ear against an upturned glass on their glass wall will be pretty conspicuous. Then I notice they've got the door wide open so they're probably not masterminding something terrible. Or else they're awful at it.

I abort this mission and try now to interrogate Martin, our beloved security guard, the eyes and ears of the building. He's busy trying to crack the National Lottery and seems quite stressed. It turns out that William Hill now do their own lottery twice day and all the winning numbers have to be input into his complex chart.

I ask him some questions but he won't reveal anything. He's too professional. I'm running out of time and am not on schedule for 137 leaks an hour.

I realise I need to get in there among the people. I need to go undercover. My first thought is to infiltrate M15. But then I worry about getting arrested and interrogated for days in a basement with an anglepoise lamp being shone in my eyes. My second thought is the government, but I have very similar worries. What other big British institution can I expose?

Then it comes to me. Marks & Spencer. I don't waste time thinking this through any further. I go straight to the giant flagship Marks & Spencer store in Marble Arch and say to the first assistant I see, "Hi, I start today, can you tell me where the staffroom is?"

The lady tells me to go to the reception and gives me directions that involve going outside then turning left, then left.

I find myself in a narrow room with two lifts and a small desk. A lady sits there, who I am immediately terrified of. She's an older, fair-haired lady and looks very no-nonsense.

I say to her, "Hi, I'm starting work here today."

I can tell she takes an immediate dislike to me. Perhaps because I'm turning up for work on my first day at two o'clock in the afternoon.

"Where are you from?" she asks.

"What do you mean?" I reply.

She says, clearly irritated, "Are you on attachment? A graduate training scheme?"

I'm not sure what this means, so I say, "Erm, I just had an interview and I start today."

"What job is it?"

"Erm. Shop floor. I think," I say, a slight tremble entering my voice.

"You think," she repeats.

"Yes," I say.

"Who's your contact here? Who were you told to ask for?"

"I can't remember. I don't know."

"You don't know," she repeats.

"No," I say.

She takes my name. I'm so embarrassed by this whole situation I give a false name. She writes it down. She doesn't spell it right but it's a false name so I don't say anything.

She tells me to take a seat and that she's going to call Corinna.

I sit down. It's got quite busy with people coming in and out so I don't hear her on the phone. But when she finishes she says, "It's definitely this branch, is it?"

"I think so," I tell her.

There's a man standing next to her. They look at each other and laugh in a very derogatory way.

I'm really insulted. I know it's my first day at work (sort of), but I'm so insulted I say, "Is something funny?"

She says, "It's just that there are two branches on Oxford Street."

Then she starts asking me questions about the interview.

"When did I have it?"

"Two weeks ago."

"Where?"

"Head office."

"Who with?"

"I can't remember."

I'm beginning to think I might have had an easier interrogation at M15 in the basement with the anglepoise lamp in my face.

Her phone's ringing now. She answers it then tells me Corinna wants to speak to me. I take the receiver. Corinna tells me she's checked with all the managers and nobody is expecting me today.

"Hmm," I say. "I'm wondering now if it wasn't Debenhams."

I look at the receptionist. She looks 50% disgusted and 50% pitying.

I put the phone down.

I say to her, "I'm wondering now if it wasn't Debenhams."

Strangely, she's now about 90% pitying. She speaks to me in a kindly way and gives me directions to the Debenhams.

I know it looks like I've failed. But I didn't! While I was waiting in reception, a man came down to speak to another man with a hard hat. I didn't catch their whole conversation, but I did hear that they're modernising lifts five and seven and I heard the words "wood panelling".

What about that? The flagship M&S are modernising their lifts and they sound really posh.

What I need to do now is leak this sensitive material.

I go back into the actual store. The first till I see has no customers but two members of staff. I say to them, "Guess what, I've just been in your reception and they're modernising lifts five and seven."

The reaction was unexpected. The girl says, "Bloody hell."

The man becomes animated, "I've been stuck in the lift twice this month."

They're really interested. The girl adds, "Perhaps now they'll do up the locker rooms," and then, "Well, that gives me something to think about."

I'm so pleased with this leakage that I try one more till. There's a man and woman again. I tell them about the lifts. They too are genuinely interested. The man says, "Those lifts break down every other day, no exaggeration." The woman agrees that it's great news. I add the snippet about the wood panelling. They don't care about that, though, they just want them to work.

I can only imagine that my lift-modernising leak is moving like wildfire through M&S. And I've just got another 1,199,999 leaks to go.

It's a new day and while I didn't manage to do 137 leaks an hour yesterday, I did do one. So I'm full of confidence and thinking about how some of the best-known WikiLeaks are the American Embassy cable ones.

I don't see any reason why I can't also uncover some secrets from a foreign embassy, by intercepting some kind of written material.

I make a list of countries that I'm a bit suspicious about. They are: Malta, Singapore, Canada, The Bahamas.

I don't want you to think I've just made a list of countries where they speak English so that I can understand the written material. Please don't think that.

I decide to focus on Canada. Their embassy is in Grosvenor Square and I walk up to the ornate doors confidently before I'm stopped by a security guard.

"Can I help you?" he asks.

"Hi, I'm from Confidential Waste Management Services. It's regarding your shredder."

"Oh, okay," he says and lets me in.

My plan is working! Surely all secrets go through a shredder. I will have to do the world's biggest jigsaw, but that's the kind of sacrifice you have to make to get to the truth.

I'm inside now and facing a lady behind glass. I tell her, "I'm from Confidential Waste Management Services. I'm doing an audit of all our shredders, so could you show me where your machine is?"

I'm not really sure what an "audit of all our machines"

93

means, but it sounds like the kind of thing that someone from Confidential Waste Management Services might say.

She wants to know if my company supplies their shredder. "Of course," I answer. This seems to be the right answer and she tries to call the person responsible, but they're not answering, and now five business people have come in with an appointment so she asks me to wait.

I watch them all go through a lengthy security procedure before they're allowed in. IDs are checked, photos taken, they walk through a body scanner, all their bags are put through a luggage scanner. It's like at an airport but they can take a full-sized shampoo in. Although for clarity, I should say I didn't see anybody try.

Meanwhile I have a look around the entrance hall. There's a guest book, which I flick through for some secrets. I find that on 16 June, Kym Marsh visited, and she tried to disguise her identity by spelling Kym with an "i" not a "y". Mysterious.

I have the idea now that I'll try hacking into their Internet and reading their emails, even though I have no idea how to do this. I get out my phone but their Wi-Fi is locked. I ask the man in charge of the scanner if he can tell me what the password is. He looks at me incredulously and then says, "No."

I don't need the Wi-Fi code now though as I've spotted a rubbish bin by his desk. What if I ask to put something in the bin and then cleverly pick something out and secrete it up my sleeve? It could reveal an amazing secret.

I pull an old rail ticket out of my coat pocket and he agrees to me putting it in the bin. I go over to it and see there's some scrunched-up paper inside. I don't let it worry me that it's paper they didn't bother to shred, maybe just some doodling or a shopping list.

I drop my ticket in and go to grab the scrunched-up paper, but he's standing right by me watching my every move and I'm not quick enough. I don't have the sleight of hand. For the first time ever I wish that David Blaine was with me.

The lady behind the glass is calling me over now. She tells me she still can't get hold of the person responsible so I need to ring and make an appointment to be able to see the shredder.

I know this is going to surprise a lot of people, but it appears you can't just walk into an embassy and then walk away with all their shredding.

It's disappointing but I decide to see what I can discover from outside the building. I'm sure there are lots of secrets accidentally visible from the outside. I walk around, trying to peer in to the windows. All the blinds are closed, which is very mysterious.

But then I see another entrance with heavy-looking, wood-panelled double doors. There's a sign on it that reads: "Deliveries between 8 a.m. and 4 p.m." I give it an experimental push. It's open. I go in. It's a room with another X-ray scanner, a big long one and also two men. A standing man and a sitting-down man.

I'm not quite sure what to say now. So, thinking on my feet, I say, "Sorry, I can't read very well, what time do you accept deliveries?"

They laugh at me a bit, which is a bit insensitive towards the semi-illiterate, and then ask me why.

"I'm sending a parcel," I tell them. They want to know if it's cake for them. "Maybe," I say.

I need to try and get some secrets so I add, "What kind of things do you usually get sent?"

They won't tell me anything. Luckily though, I've had a brilliant idea. "If I bring you some cake, will you tell me a brilliant top secret?"

They agree, telling me their favourite is chocolate cake and I promise that I'll be back tomorrow.

It's the next day, I've got the cake (chocolate mini rolls. I'm sure Julian Assange bought leaks with 99p sweet baked goods) and I'm back outside the Canadian Embassy delivery door.

There's a queue today, but I walk straight in with confidence. I've got an assignation.

I see that sitting man is the same but standing man is different.

"Hi, it's me again!" I say to sitting man. "Do you remember me?"

Sitting man doesn't seem that happy to see me.

"Guess what I've got for you!" I exclaim.

He doesn't look excited. New standing man just looks confused. I pull the chocolate mini rolls out of my bag.

"You can tell me a secret now," I say conspiratorially.

Sitting man is becoming flustered. He says to new standing man, "It wasn't me, it was Alfonso. I didn't promise."

I am worried now that new standing man is actually his boss. I check but he's not. Then someone else walks in. He's wearing a long coat. They don't need to tell me, I already know.

"Here's our boss now."

New standing man leaves the room. He clearly wants nothing to do with this. But this could be the lead I'm looking for. I decide to try and get some secrets out of boss man.

I start by asking if I can go through the big long scanner. It's a no.

"Have you had anything suspect go through there?" I ask.

"Yes, a few times," he says.

I ask them what they do with it and they show me a big machine. It's like a giant metal beer barrel that can contain an explosion.

I'm asking so many questions that they start to get suspicious and ask me if I'm M15. I'm thrilled.

Then they put my chocolate mini rolls through the scanner. They really are suspicious. But I can't give up. I beg them for a secret and get nothing.

I briefly consider asking for my mini rolls back, then leave. Without them.

I know it looks like I achieved nothing at all at the Canadian Embassy. But what if sitting man behind the delivery door had told me a secret so big that I couldn't repeat it, or even say I knew it because it could topple several governments? Let alone write about it in a book. Consider that possibility. I'll say no more.

It's the final day and I feel ready to leak the shocking secrets of the rich and famous. And I know exactly which two uber-rich and famous celebrities to tackle.

Noel Sullivan, formerly of Hear'Say, and the girl who came third in BBC TV talent contest *Over the Rainbow*. This decision was based entirely on their high level of wealth and celebrity, and not that they are both starring in the musical *Grease* at the theatre right by my work.

I feel like the best place to uncover secrets is the stage door, but it's not immediately obvious where it is, so I go into the booking office and ask the man in the booth.

"Oh," says booth man, "Are you here for a meeting with Tamsin?"

I immediately say, "Yes." This could be the key to any number of secrets. Then he goes to pick up the phone, presumably to call Tamsin, and I panic.

I blurt out, "I'm not really. I'm lying."

He's really confused and still has the receiver in his hand.

"So, sorry, you are or you aren't here to see Tamsin?"

"I'm not. I was lying."

It's extremely embarrassing. And I still don't know where the stage door is. I add, "I just wanted to know where the stage door is."

He tells me and I walk round to find you can't access the actual door because of a big metal gate. But there's an intercom system, so I press the buzzer.

A man answers. I say, "Hello. I'm doing a project on West End stars. Could I come and ask some questions?"

The voice replies, "I'm sorry. I'm not allowed to speak."

This is puzzling. He is speaking. I politely don't mention this and instead say, "So you can't answer any questions?"

He says he's not allowed to. He's clearly been hushed up. He's probably been given hush money. What is going on in there? Something, I'm sure of it. But I can't find out any more.

I move on to another theatre nearby. At this stage door, I get to see the face of the man I'm talking to. I tell him I'm doing a project on West End stars and he reluctantly agrees to answer some questions.

I plan something very clever. I'll ask him several bland, innocuous questions to give him a false sense of security.

Then hit him with the killer question when he's so relaxed he answers without thinking. It goes like this:

"What time do the stars arrive?"

"Has anyone ever been really late?"

"Do they bring their own lunch with them?"

"Has one of the stars ever murdered anyone?"

Unbelievably it doesn't work.

I'm feeling really down and I can't stop thinking about the first theatre where the stage-door man was told he wasn't allowed to speak. I'm desperate to know what's going on there. I need to go back and I can try again because he hasn't seen my face. All I'd need to do is disguise my voice.

There's a slight problem in that I'm not great at accents. I could probably make a better stab at brain surgery than convince someone I'm American, for example.

But I press the buzzer again and say in an American accent, "Hi, I'm here to clean the dressing rooms."

I have an anxious wait of around one second before the man says, "Okay. I'll open the gate for you."

The gate is now automatically opening. I enter, walk a little way down a pathway and then through the stage door. There are two men behind a counter.

"Hi, I'm here to clean the dressing rooms," I drawl in an accent that's somewhere between American and Welsh but not recognisable as either.

"What's the name of your cleaning company?" one man asks.

"CCC," I tell him. "Cleaning Company Services." I quickly realise my mistake and add, "They spell services with a C."

The man says, "Okay, I'll just check."

He speaks to someone on the phone and then hands it to

me. It's another man. He wants to know my cleaning company name and tells me that's not the one they use. I ask him which one they do use but he won't tell me.

I can't leave yet though. I ask to use their Wi-Fi so I can check I'm at the right place.

One of the men says, "No," but his accompanying facial expression suggests he actually meant to say, "Are you insane? Of course you can't use our Wi-Fi. Can you please now leave."

I start reading the signing-in book. It's a bit of an awkward moment. I've been exposed as someone pretending to be their cleaner but I've still not left and the men are staring at me.

There are no famous people signed in to the book but I do see that someone came in this week to fix a leak.

Then I hear a woman singing "You're the One That I Want" to a piano accompaniment.

"Is that the girl who came third on *Over the Rainbow*?" I ask excitedly.

They tell me it isn't as she's left the show now.

My eyes widen. "Under difficult circumstances?" I ask.

"No," they say.

"Who's that singing then?" They won't tell me. My mind is racing. Who could it be? My best guess from the sound of her voice is Samantha Cameron.

I think they really want me to go as they're saying, "The door is just over there."

I leave and reflect on what I've achieved, which is not quite 137 leaks an hour. Close though. Pretty close.

11

The Challenge:
To become a top model

"You know full well I could never become a model. This is the most insane task you've ever set."

I'm thirty-six and five foot three with bandy legs and a double chin.

Geoff has some advice though. "Just practise balancing a book on your head so you get your poise right."

I'm worried he's getting modelling confused with graduating from Swiss finishing school.

I don't know anything about modelling. Yes, I watch the modelling TV shows, but I'm not sure how representative of the industry they are. In the last series of *Britain's Next Top Model* there tended to be a lot of naked and faux-lesbian shoots.

I do know that supermodels say things like, "I don't get out of bed for less than ten thousand dollars a day." Whereas I got out of bed for £7 a week for six years when I was a papergirl. I need some advice from famous models.

I go to the renowned Select modelling agency. I've no plan as such, but surely models will be going in and out all day, and I've brought some rice cakes with me as an icebreaker.

I stand outside. After a very long time, I see a really tall, thin, blonde girl coming out, who is very obviously a model. She's also very obviously about thirteen and with her parents. I start feeling a bit seedy.

Maybe this isn't the best place. I try another agency. They look after Gisele, Lara Stone and Miranda Kerr, so maybe they'll all be there being weighed and having their hair length measured and things like that.

As I approach I see a real-life model having his photo taken outside. It's very exciting. I stand and watch. It's a male model with pillarbox-red hair and he's just posing against a wall.

I'm trying to think of a way to start up a conversation.

"Why don't you try putting your hand against your face?" I suggest.

Both the model and the photographer laugh. I'm surprised. It's a great idea. I've seen this done on the modelling TV shows loads of times.

But at least I've got his attention. So now I offer him a rice cake.

"I've already eaten," he says, like I was offering him lunch. Very telling.

I need to come straight to the point so I ask him outright for some modelling advice.

"Be natural," he tells me, and politely doesn't add, "Grow taller, get younger, have your legs straightened."

There's a bit of a silence now, so I break it with, "Do you want to open a burger bar with me?"

He looks at me blankly, so I add, "You know, like when Naomi Campbell, Elle Macpherson, Claudia Schiffer and Christy Turlington opened the Fashion Cafe."

He doesn't remember that. Now would be the time to just leave it there but I don't. I say, "It's just that I'm looking for another model to open this burger bar with me."

He's very polite. "Sounds interesting," he says.

"Have you got funds to finance it with?" I ask.

He doesn't. I feel like the conversation really is over now. The photographer has been fiddling with her camera throughout. I really want to ask her to take my photo but feel too shy.

I know this is weird. That I can ask a stranger if they want to open a burger bar with me but I can't ask a photographer to take my photo. It shows how far I've got to go to become a model.

I have to go now and put some money on my flat's electricity meter key. I'm sure Kate Moss often has to go off and do this.

But I've got advice: be natural. The next step in becoming a top model is to get an agent. However, being thirty-six and five foot three, there is strong potential for humiliation.

I need to build confidence. I turn to my boyfriend. He must find me attractive in some way. I ask him, "Do you think I could be a model?"

He replies immediately. "Yes!" There's a pause. Then he adds, "A hand model."

I'm strangely thrilled by this answer. I had no idea I had such nice hands.

"Do you really think I could be a hand model?" I ask him.

He snorts. "No. I was joking."

It's now I recall something my mum once said to me when I was twelve. My secondary school, Westcliff High, held a charity week every year. One of the fundraising events was a Miss Westcliff competition. *Miss World* was a must-watch TV show then. It was the eighties; different times. I'd told my mum I'd entered. There was a long silence. Then she said, "Well, of course *I* think you're very pretty, darling."

With all this going round my head, I go off to get myself a supermodel agent.

I'm at one of the most famous agencies in the Covent Garden area: Premier Model Management. It's described as "The original pioneers behind 'supermodel' branding".

I'm nervous. For many reasons. But I can do something about two of them: my age and my height.

Firstly, I can lie about my age. Models are really young. So I opt for seventeen. More than half my age. I got away with it before in the youth club. In that nobody bothered to challenge me. Secondly, I know a way I can look taller.

I arrive, open the door and walk in on my tiptoes. To the right is big table where all the bookers appear to be sitting. Nobody looks up so I announce myself with a "Hello!" Just one person looks up. A man.

"Hi, I'd like help being a supermodel," I say to him.

He laughs faintly. I don't. He then looks a bit confused and directs me over to a receptionist a bit further up the room. She sends me over to a seated area opposite.

After a short while the receptionist comes over. "Okay. How old are you?"

"Thirt—" I start saying my real age. It's a terrible error. But I cover it up well with, "Well, I was thirteen a few years ago but now I'm seventeen."

There is no discernible reaction to this. "And how tall are you?" she asks.

"I'm five foot six, five foot seven." It's probably good to be a bit vague in this area.

"Okay," she says. "I'll get someone to come and see you."

I wait a bit longer. Then the man by the door – the one I originally spoke to – comes to sit with me.

"How can I help you?" he asks.

I tell him again that I want to be a supermodel. I get asked again how old I am. This time I get it right. "Seventeen," I say with confidence.

"And how tall are you?" he asks. Before I get a chance to answer he says, "Well, let's measure you."

It's quite possible that he's pre-empting another lie. He takes me round the back to a tape measure fixed to a wall. I'm still on tiptoes. I'm pushing myself up as high as I can.

"Oh," he says. "Just five foot five. We can't take you."

I really wish I had bigger toes. I try not to sound desperate as I say, "Oh, that's okay, I don't want to do catwalk. I've got bandy legs. And I've got blisters at the moment. I could do beauty."

"We don't do just beauty," he says quickly.

I can't leave it there. I can't just give up. I ask, "How can I get taller?"

"I don't know," the man says.

"I'll come back when I've got taller."

He was really lovely to me. But I've not been taken on. Now

I'm thinking, *Do I really need an agent?* Maybe I can go out and become a supermodel and get supermodel jobs on my own.

I head to New Bond Street with all the fancy stores that employ top models in their campaigns and go into Mulberry. I'm short, but I can model a handbag. I have a wander round until I find one that I think I can work well with. It's plum-coloured, with a short hand strap.

In the window, there's a display of two headless manne-quins alongside a fake tree with fake birds on it. There's a lady who works there standing by the door.

I move towards the display holding the plum-coloured handbag. I get right in with the headless mannequins and strike a pose. I put my left hand on my hip and my other hand has the bag hanging off my wrist. My head is to one side and I'm doing a "smize". This is smiling with the eyes, as recom-mended by Tyra Banks on *America's Next Top Model*.

Nobody stops me. People stare. A small crowd gathers, if two girls constitute a small crowd. The sun is pouring through the windows and I am starting to get hot and achy in my pose.

After about five minutes I can hear muffled talking behind me. A man appears by my side.

"Are you okay there?"

"Yeah, I'm a model. A Mulberry model."

"Oh, okay," he says.

I keep posing. I hear more muffled talking behind me. After another minute, there's a woman beside me.

"Do you have a note for this?"

I'm thinking, *What, from my mum?*

She continues with, "A note from head office?"

I tell her, "No, they just sent me here without a note."

She gestures over to the first person who spoke to me and asks him to call head office.

"What's your name?" she asks.

"Annabel Port," I tell her.

I'm a bit worried about this man calling head office with my name, but the lady is speaking again. "Can you step away from the window while we're calling?"

"Oh," I reply. "But I get paid by the hour."

She tells me to take a seat over in the folly. I have no idea what she means as we're in a shop, not some stately home gardens. She points to an area in the middle of the shop floor, a circle with seats around the outside. It's kind of a fence. It's probably the closest she can get to a cage in this situation.

I head there saying, "Okay, well, I'll keep modelling."

I sit down and model the handbag. I'm waiting a while. The staff are really staring at me. After a time, a man I've not seen before sits next to me. He says, "Annabel, who sent you?"

"Head office," I tell him.

"Got a name?"

I say the first one that comes into my head. "Christine."

"There's lots of Christines at head office," he tells me. *Really?* I think.

"Got a surname?"

"No."

"And are you from an agency?"

"Yes, I've come from Premier Model Management." This is not a lie. This is exactly where I've just come from. "Have they not got confirmation from head office yet?" I ask.

"Just trying now," he says. "It's just that sometimes the communication isn't great between head office and us, so that might be the problem."

This is a very generous-hearted and polite man. Unless he's actually starting to believe me, which means that if they can't get hold of head office I'll be stuck here holding a plum-coloured handbag all afternoon. He goes off again and I keep posing.

After another five minutes he's back with the news that there's no Christine at head office, which is strange as before he'd said there were lots. He asks to see my time sheet. I tell him I don't have one. I'm also not sure that any supermodels have time sheets.

Then it gets worse. "I tell you what," he says, getting his mobile out of his pocket, "Let's call your agency to find out what's going on."

"No!" I practically shout. "Actually, I've got to go as I think I've left the oven on."

I get out of there quickly. But it's undeniable that I did model for Mulberry. And I'm sure top models are always popping into shops for an unplanned, impromptu shop-window modelling session. So today I was a top model. And not one person mentioned my double chin.

12

The Challenge: To create some conceptual art

The winner of the Turner Prize is about to be announced, and who hasn't looked at conceptual art and thought, I could do that? Actually, I haven't.

I don't have any artistic abilities. Apart from yesterday, when I drew quite a good horse's head by following the outline of a kite shape. That's probably not enough, though.

I look to works from this year's Turner Prize shortlist for inspiration. Here's what I saw:

- Painting of a shed
- Scrunched-up bit of paper
- Some hung-up polythene
- A thing
- Another thing
- One more thing
- Hanging projectors and pictures of bits of the body

I don't feel inspired. But I'm reminded of the time I went with my parents to Tate Modern and my dad was complaining that he didn't like the art and my mum said, "Your lack of enjoyment isn't the artist's failure, it's your failure."

I try harder and I look at the winner, Martin Boyce's work. It includes a wonky bin and I am quite excited by that as we used to have them at work. Bins that were on a strange slant. When Jeremy Kyle did a late-night show here, he once complained about them in a DJ meeting. And the bins went the next day. The power this man wielded, even back then.

The wonky bin piece of art is called, *Do words have voices?*

I can't help thinking that what's happened here is that he started with the title and worked backwards. I'm not sure how he got to the bin.

But it seems that in conceptual art, that the idea is the most important aspect. That it's all about expressing yourself. I haven't really expressed myself since around 1978.

I think really hard and admit to myself that something I'm finding difficult at the moment, is keeping on top of my to-do list. I feel a bit overwhelmed by everything that I've not done yet. Like pick up all the post and junk mail from my doormat before it starts becoming difficult to open the door, get a pension and formulate any kind of career plan.

With this in mind, I come up with my title, *Silencing the List – how long is a moment?* I don't really know what I mean by the second bit but I think that's pretty standard in this world.

I get to work. I've got an A4-sized wallpaper sample that I sent off for when there was a six-second period of my life when I thought I had the energy and enthusiasm to redecorate my living room. I take this and clip a small reading light to it. Then I write on it: *sort mortgage, register at doctor's, council tax, gas bill, pay in cheque, sort accounts, get bed sheet.*

Then I stick some things on it. An AA battery, a penny, a travel sickness band, some tinfoil and a rice cake, which I've glued some M&Ms and painkillers on. Then I attach it all to a free magazine to make it a bit sturdier.

I show it to Geoff. While he's looking at it, I blow in his ear as that's part of the whole experience. He mistakes the tinfoil for some wraps of heroin and says that it looks like what a GCSE student would do if asked to create some conceptual art. I wasn't good enough to do GCSE art, so this is a big compliment for me.

I want some more feedback so I take it out on to the streets of London. On Oxford Street, there a man standing outside John Lewis. I ask him if I could show him some art I've created.

He reluctantly agrees. I pull it out of the bag. Unfortunately, several painkillers and M&Ms have fallen off the rice cake.

As he's looking at it, I start to blow into his ear, or rather the side of his head as he's wearing a woolly hat.

He doesn't respond, so I blow harder. Still nothing. I ask him what he thinks of my art.

"It's nice," he says.

I can't get anything else out of him.

I decide to try someone else. I need to try and fix the art first though. I don't know if you've ever been down on your hands and knees supergluing painkillers and M&Ms to a rice cake on Oxford Street in the run-up to Christmas, but it's not great. I wonder if Tracy Emin has ever found herself doing this.

Once I'm ready, I approach a middle-aged woman with a blonde bob.

"Oh, I don't know about art," she protests. But she takes it and starts to really stare. I begin blowing towards her ear. It's covered by her hair but I can see her hair moving. I do about five blows in a row before she turns to me and says, "What are you doing?"

"It's part of the art experience," I tell her.

"But what is it?" she asks.

"It's my art."

"But what is it?" she asks again.

I'm not getting anywhere so I say, "How does it make you feel?"

"What is going on?" she says.

I wasn't expecting this level of confusion. She tells me now that her daughter is much better at these things and then, right on cue, and I suspect much to her relief, she spots her.

The daughter has a better response. "Well, for me it's about drugs. The pills and the tinfoil for crack cocaine and then there's the energy for the battery and penny for the cost."

"What about the travel sickness band?" I ask.

"Oh, I thought that was a doorbell," says the mum.

I'm starting to worry that it does look a bit druggy. I rip the tinfoil off. And give up trying to glue the M&Ms and pain-killers on to the rice cake. I feel like it's missing something now so I add an audio element. I record the sound of me crying on my phone. Now it's ready to be seen by the wider public. At a gallery.

It's important to find the right place. I spend quite a lot of time researching all the different galleries in London and which ones would be the best suited to my style of artwork, and then I pick the one that's closest to my work with free admission. The Tate Modern.

It takes me a while to find the best floor to display my art. It wouldn't look right with paintings. It needs other conceptual art. On the fifth floor, there is an exhibition called *Energy and Process*. This could be a great fit.

I'm in a room with about five other exhibits. They are quite big ones. There's a large bit of canvas draped round a glass. Some long twigs leaning against the wall. A black foam sculpture. Between these two last things is a gap. There's just white walls and grey floor, crying out for something special.

I try to lean my work against the wall but it keeps slipping down. I put a plastic bag under it. Then I realise a sign would be a good idea. I rip some paper out of my notebook and write: "*Silencing the List – how long is a moment?* by Annabel Port." I step back and wait for the crowds to flock.

In no time at all, a man is coming over to have a look. I press play on the sound of me crying then start blowing in his ear. He gives me a bemused look but tells me it's "nice". It's clear you can get away with a lot in a modern art gallery.

Then it goes very quiet. Nobody else comes over. Perhaps as they're put off by the ear-blowing. I'm forced to say to a girl looking at the art next to mine, "Come and have a look at this one."

"Interesting," she says. "It's like from school."

I'm worried she means primary school but she goes on with, "Yes, like emotions from school."

This is a very deep reading into my work.

I make someone else come and have a look. This man says,

"It's very different to everything else here." I take that as a compliment.

It's still really quiet. Then I realise why. All the other works of art are roped off, while mine looks like someone's just dumped some of their stuff there for a bit.

I have an idea. I take my scarf off and use it to cordon off my art.

It works a treat. It's a real turning point. I'll look back on that moment as when my artwork really took off.

Lots of people are coming to look now. At one point, there are six people crowding round. I don't see this happen to any other exhibits in this room or in any other room. Maybe the other artists should consider ear-blowing and using a scarf as a cordon.

I've been here about twenty minutes now and nobody has tried to stop me from exhibiting my own stuff at Tate Modern.

A young woman with piercings comes to look at it twice. She really studies it. Two women have a really good look and say twice, "It's really cool." A man calls it "interesting".

And then something bad happens. A man in suit comes up to me and barks, "Is this yours?"

"Yes," I tell him. There's a small chance he's a billionaire businessman wanting to snap up my work for a small fortune.

He's not.

"You can't exhibit your work here."

He's not friendly.

"It's been really popular though," I tell him.

"Just take it away."

"What do you think of it?" I ask.

"I've got no opinion, just take it away."

I'm wondering if he's in the right job. I'm a bit scared of him though so I don't say this, I pack up my stuff and leave.

But for half an hour today, I really did have my conceptual art exhibited at Tate Modern.

Q&A 1

Questions you might be asking yourself

You might have some questions at this stage. Other than, *Why am I reading this book?* Here I will answer them. They are not real questions from real people. I just made them up. So I will basically be talking to myself, but I've done far weirder things, as you'll now already know.

Was your life really that boring before you started doing all these things?
I am pretty boring. But some exciting things happened to me pre-challenges. I counted them and there are seven.

1. I once found a mushroom that looked like ET in a bowl of Thai food. It really looked remarkably like ET. Tragically, I didn't take a photo of it. This was before camera phones, when you just had to take people's word for it. So you'll just have to take my word for it. I was so excited

that I called the waiter over to show him. But for some reason he took it as a complaint and took the mushroom away, which was fine as I never could've eaten it. But I do occasionally google "mushroom ET" to check he's not taken it on tour and made millions out of it.

2. I was once held hostage by a pigeon in the greeting cards shop, Cards Galore.

3. When we were little, my sister and I won goldfish at a fair. (Different times.) My sister called hers Finny; mine was called Fanny, after a character in an Enid Blyton book. This wasn't the exciting bit (although it might be for some of you). The exciting bit was that one day, Fanny the goldfish tried to commit suicide by jumping out of the bowl. Luckily, I got there in time and was able to tell her (might have been a him) that he/she had so much to live for and put him/her back in the bowl. It's the closest I've ever got to being the angel in *It's a Wonderful Life*.

4. I got cautioned for busking when I was twelve. My friend Sally and I were singing on Southend High Street with a hat at our feet. It was during our goth phase so one of us always had a hat. We sang "Those Magnificent Men in Their Flying Machines". I don't know how two twelve-year-olds knew this song from a 1965 film. But I do know that it would've been nice to hear two pre-teens, dressed as goths, singing about being frightfully keen and going up tiddly up up and down tiddly down down. Maybe this is what softened the policewoman into a caution rather than an arrest.

5. When I was thirteen, I met the presenter Caron Keating at a fete, and she said she liked my cardigan.

6. On holiday in Gozo, Malta, I sat two tables away from *The Apprentice*'s Margaret Mountford and witnessed her ask for a doggy bag at the end of her meal.

7. When I was eleven, I had my pen-pal request printed in *Smash Hits* magazine's RSVP section. If you're under twenty-five, a pen pal was someone you may or may not have met, and who you communicated with only by letter. It's like having a Twitter or Facebook friend but involving a lot more envelopes. *Smash Hits* had a section where you could ask for pen pals. I feel about 100 years old even writing these words. Anyway, I had my request printed. I can still remember it word for word. "I'm a desperate eleven-year-old seeking fans of A-ha, Five Star and Falco." Desperate! That's a nice, un-needy word. I received hundreds of letters, including one from someone called Trevor who drew a picture of the female genitalia. A very detailed picture. I flushed it down the toilet. I only wrote back to one of the letters. They never replied.

That's pretty much it. You see Geoff's point.

But you've worked in radio. Isn't that exciting?
I'd describe my time working in radio as 90% crying over a blank piece of paper.

Oh. That doesn't sound all that great. Well, at least you did these challenges. You did do all these things, right? Actually do them?
This is a question that I really have been asked. My answer is that it's easier to do the challenges than go to the brain-taxing effort of making it up. (See the Introduction for how lazy I

am.) Also, the reality is often more surprising and strange than anything my imagination could ever conjure up.

How long do you have to do them? It's just that you don't always seem to achieve very much, no offence.
None taken. Usually three days. But not all day for three days. So about three hours in total.

Okay, that makes sense. One thing that really concerns me is the length of time you claim to have done a paper round. Did you really do one from the age of twelve to eighteen? As that seems quite weird, no offence.
None taken. I know what you mean. Doing a paper round at twelve is actually illegal and at eighteen it probably should be illegal. I only stopped then as my mum said she'd give me the equivalent money if I gave it up. She said it was because she wanted me to concentrate on my upcoming A-level exams. But looking back, I think she was just embarrassed by me.

You've mentioned rice cakes twice now and other stuff that makes me worried about your diet. Do you eat properly? As it seems that you don't, no offence.
Some taken. I did go through a phase of eating rice cakes but that was only because I was too lazy to make toast. I'm a bit less lazy now. I've also cut down on my Bendicks Bittermint habit.

We are twelve challenges in. What have you learned about yourself and others so far?
What do you think this is, a self-help book? I've got no life lessons for you. I've learned nothing.

Come on, there must be something.

Okay, if I must.

1. Strangers are often so incredibly polite. Like when I was trying to get someone to drop litter and they declined, saying, "It's a good idea though." It was terrible idea!
2. It's easy to lie about your age because nobody will contradict you. People are terrified of getting ages wrong. Tell everyone you are eighty-two or twelve. They might look surprised but they won't dare call you a liar.
3. 50% of security guards are lovely.
4. You can get away with a lot if you just do it. I exhibited my work in Tate Modern. It was only for about half an hour, but I did it. All artists should do the same, then they can put it on their CV. If artists have CVs. They probably don't.
5. I have no shame.

13

The Challenge: To write a biography of Simon Cowell

The news is full of Simon Cowell at the moment. An unauthorised biography has just been published and there's clearly a
big appetite for all the salacious details. The affair with Dannii
Minogue (boring), the regular colonics, vitamin injections
and Botox (dull, dull and dull) and the fact he only uses black
toilet paper (best news story ever).

I didn't even know you could get black toilet paper. It can't
be a very good visual aid when it comes to judging the effi-
ciency of your wiping. Plus, it's not good if you ever want to
dress up as an Egyptian mummy. But, I suppose it would be
handy if you ever need to make a quick gimp mask.

It's clear to me that the biography of Simon Cowell got
published on the strength of this one fact and that it's going to
be very difficult to top this revelation. Still, I won't let it stop
me from capitalising on the current fascination with this man
and write my own unofficial biography. Besides, this book

was out last Friday so it's not very up to date. I can get some much more recent revelations. And, by luck, I already have a big lead.

Yesterday, Mark, a work colleague, had been passing by a theatre in Soho when he saw Simon Cowell get out of a huge Bentley and go into a doorway by the theatre, surrounded by a harem of screaming teenage girls. This last detail sounds like an exaggeration but that's not the important bit. What was he doing there?

I make my way to this theatre and start studying the doorways. One has got a company called The Shed marked on it. Perhaps Simon Cowell is buying a shed. I could dedicate a whole chapter to this in my biography.

I press the intercom button for The Shed.

"Hi, delivery," I say in an attempt to get buzzed in. It works.

I go up to the reception and say to the man there, "Hi, was Simon in yesterday?"

He seems to have forgotten about this delivery I'm supposed to be making and says, "Erm, why? I mean, yes, he was here."

He's being quite cautious. At first. Until he forgets and admits the truth. Maybe it's a secret shed. A shed where secret, unspeakable things happen. My biography is really starting to shape up. But I need more details. I need a way in so I think on my feet and say, "It's just that I think he left his umbrella behind here yesterday and I've been sent to get it."

"Oh, okay," he says, takes my name, then picks up the phone.

It's now that I notice a *Britain's Got Talent* form on his desk. This is not a shed company.

I hear him say, "I've got Annabel who works for Simon here. Did he leave an umbrella up there yesterday?"

He puts the phone down and says, "Okay, I'll get someone to take you up to Edit Suite nine."

This is exactly what happens. I'm being taken to an edit suite. An edit suite where they are editing *Britain's Got Talent*. I can see it on the screen. Or rather, they were editing. They are now looking for an umbrella. One man is lifting up sofa cushions. Another asks me what it looks like. I tell him it's red. I'm sure Simon Cowell is a red umbrella kind of guy.

I'm pretending to look for this imaginary umbrella too, but really I'm looking for something amazing for my biography.

Then one of them says, "I don't remember him having an umbrella."

I'm very worried about being caught in a lie and feel a bit bad that these stressed-looking men are hunting for an imaginary umbrella so I say, "Oh well, perhaps he left it somewhere else," and I leave. But I've already made a great start on my first chapter and I've got an idea as to where I can get some more material.

I go to the newsagent over the road and say, "Hi, can I get Simon Cowell's usual order please?"

They have no idea what I mean. Disappointingly, he doesn't appear to have a tab at the local newsagent. Either that or they are more adept at protecting Simon's privacy.

But I'm ready now to write my first chapter from my unauthorised biography. It's all about Simon's career.

Chapter 1: Career

On Monday 23 April, Simon Cowell went into Soho to do some editing on *Britain's Got Talent*. It was raining but he didn't bring an umbrella with him. He did some editing with some stressed-looking men and then went somewhere else. He didn't buy anything from the newsagent's, in fact he never buys anything at all from the local newsagent's.

I'm very happy with this and confident about the next chapters as I have two more leads.

A long time ago, when the radio station had a different name, a woman came in to reception who I immediately recognised. She was a model in magazines like *Just Seventeen* that I read when I was young. It emerged that she was a friend of Charlotte, who worked in PR.

A few years later I recognised the model again. As being Simon Cowell's girlfriend, Terri Seymour.

Charlotte left ages ago, but if I can get in contact with her again, I'm sure I can extract all kinds of information about Simon's love life. Like maybe he did use that black toilet paper to fashion a quick and easy gimp mask.

I do some googling. Charlotte has since changed her surname, but with skills that I'm amazed M15 haven't yet tried to utilise, I manage to find her work email.

I send her a message. I should mention at this point that while she was a high-flying executive at the company, I was doing little more than work experience.

Hi Charlotte,

I used to work with you at Virgin Radio (many years ago). I was a runner but now I'm a presenter with Geoff Lloyd on Absolute Radio.

Hope you are well. I was wondering if you were still friends with Terri Seymour and if you had an email address for her.

Many thanks,

Annabel

I don't beat around the bush with any friendly anecdotes about the old days, mainly as I don't have any. So I'm amazed that less than an hour later I get a response.

She starts with:

> What a blast from the past.

I'm pretty sure she's lying and has no memory of me but this is very polite.

Then she goes on with:

> I'm afraid I don't know where she is. I did see her
> a couple of times when she was with Simon Cowell. I
> presumed she was in LA, but maybe not.

I'm a little overwhelmed by all this information but I manage to pull it together into a coherent chapter about Simon and love. Here it is:

Chapter 2: Love

Simon Cowell went out with Terri Seymour for a bit. During that time, she was still friends with a girl called Charlotte but they are not friends any more and Charlotte doesn't know where she is. She might be in LA.

It's now time to follow my second lead.

Geoff and I have a mutual friend named Suzanne, who used to work at the same record company as Simon Cowell. I get in contact with her, begging for titbits for my biography. She does not let me down.

She tells me that she used to work in the floor below Simon. She was often carrying big piles of CDs and merchandise around and Simon was the only man who would hold the door open for her. He was a complete gentleman and this was at the height of *Pop Idol*.

Also, she said that when Will Young won *Pop Idol* he was brought to spend the day at the offices to learn about what everybody did. I love it that he had to do this. He'd just won a £1 million recording contract but he still had to do what essentially sounds like a day of work experience in the office.

Anyway, on that day, Will spent ages in Suzanne's department, which specialised in back catalogue and reissues, as that's where his musical heart lay. Plus, it was the only place that didn't have pop and R'n'B pumping from the stereos. Later on, there was a presentation in their company bar. Simon introduced Will and congratulated him on his recent success, then handed the mic to him. Will waxed lyrical about how wonderful Suzanne's division was and how Zen her offices were. Simon's face was a picture. She said she often sees him pull the same face when Louis puts a novelty act through on *The X Factor*.

This all gives me two new chapters:

Chapter 3: Manners
Simon Cowell has been a very polite man in his life and always holds doors open for ladies. He is a gentleman.

Chapter 4: Will Young
Simon Cowell wishes Gareth Gates had won *Pop Idol*.

I'm a little worried now that this is stuff from ten years ago. I need something much more recent, so I think back to *Britain's Got Talent*. The live shows start in around ten days. This gives me an idea. I find out where they are filmed and I ring the studios.

"Hi, this is Annabel. I'm calling from Simon Cowell's office."

The woman says, "Oh, hello. How is Simon?"

"Oh, you know, his usual self," I say jovially.

The lady asks how she can help me and I say I have a few things I need to check facilities-wise regarding the upcoming live shows.

"Oh, I'll put you through to the client liaison manager," she says.

There's now another woman on the line saying cheerfully, "Hello, Annabel."

"Hi," I say. "I've just got a few very quick questions for you. Simon's dressing room, what colour are the walls in there?"

"I think they're cream. Hold on."

I hear her say, "Harry, what colour are the walls in Simon's dressing room?" I hear his reply of "whitish". Then she comes back on the line and splits the difference with, "Yes, they're a whitish cream."

"Right," I say, "Sorry about this, but is there any chance of them being painted baby blue?"

She laughs. I don't.

"Oh well, I'll ask our maintenance guys. Hang on, I'll just check."

I'm put on hold. After a while she comes back. "When would you need it done by?"

I tell her next week.

"Right, well, the room's being set by Monday, but do you think Tuesday will be okay?"

"Tuesday will be great," I tell her.

I move on to the catering now and tell her that Simon has especially requested the herbal Purdey drink in the silver bottle.

That seems to be fine.

"One more thing," I say. "The toilets, I'm just checking they're all really clean and definitely have a toilet brush by the bowl."

"Well, obviously Simon's got his own toilet that we don't go into. We're not allowed. It's as he left it."

"Right, yes of course. Well that's all great. Speak to you soon."

That's my fifth chapter sorted:

Chapter 5: Britain's Got Talent

Simon has his own dressing room at the Fountain Studios. The walls are a whitish cream but were changed to baby blue on Tuesday 1 May. He drank that Purdey drink. Simon has his own toilet at the studios and nobody else is allowed to go in at any point at all. I think we all know why.

All I need to do now is get it all serialised in the *Sun*. I send all the chapters to their news desk and wait for the big headlines, while having a lovely daydream about Simon liking it all so much that he wants it for his own autobiography. Then I remember the toilet bit and the daydream ends. Still, I hope he likes his new baby-blue walls.

14

The Challenge: To get revenge

I'm very sure that there are a lot of people who I need to exact my revenge on. I start making a list:

1. My upstairs neighbour, who complained that I turned my taps on too loudly.
2. My upstairs neighbours in my last place, who regularly flooded my flat.
3. Mr Tsang, my second-year senior form teacher, who wrote in my school report that I was "moody" and "rude". I was a teenager. Of course I was moody and rude.
4. Tim, for dumping me aged twelve after we'd been on a date to a tropical-fish shop.
5. Mark, who broke up with me at thirteen for a girl he went on to marry, so actually I'll forgive him.
6. Dave, who dumped me at fourteen after arranging to meet me outside WHSmith's on Southend High Street at

1 p.m. and just never turned up. I waited for an hour. This was way before mobile phones.

7. Tristan, who broke up with me at fifteen. I rang up his house and he answered in a normal voice and then when he heard it was me, he pretended to be his mum in a high-pitched voice and said he was out.

8. Ian, who broke up with me in my twenties by just never calling or texting me again.

9. Jon, who did exactly the same as Ian.

10. Another Jon, who ended things on my birthday, at my birthday party and didn't buy me a present.

11. The former actress and presenter Daisy Donovan, who I did work experience with at the BBC before she got a bit famous. She got all the best jobs and everyone really sucked up to her because of her famous family. Admittedly, that wasn't really her fault.

12. The girl who kept changing her mind about buying my last flat.

13. The Labour Party canvasser who came to my door, was sick on the doorstep and then knocked and tried to get me to vote Labour. I had to clear it up with a hangover.

14. Lord Sugar for never replying to any of my many tweets to him.

15. Anyone who puts their bag on a seat in a crowded London Underground carriage.

16. The boy in 1986 who said I couldn't sing.

17. The manager of the Music and Video Exchange, who sacked me after a few days and I'm still not even really sure why. There were complaints about the angle that I stapled some paper though.

18. The man selling single red roses in Sicily, who, after I

declined to purchase one, hissed at me every time he saw me.

19. Warwick University for not letting me on a course even though I had more A-level points than they'd asked for. They said the letters were in the wrong order or something.

It's quite a lengthy list. I probably haven't got time to do them all as I've only got three days. It seems that there are a lot of men who have spurned me over the years, though. I could really get my teeth into this and do all the things you're supposed to do, like sew prawns into their curtain hems.

Another revenge method is cutting off one sleeve of all their suits but a) I'm not convinced that the type of person I've ever gone out with would own more than one suit and b) in the intervening twenty-five years since my first rejection, I've found that the passion and fury have faded past the stage where I'd want to track him down, break into his house and hack his clothes to bits.

I go back to the list and realise I'm still pretty annoyed with Warwick University for not letting me on my course even though I had more A-level points than they'd asked for. I'm going to exact my revenge on them!

My first thought is a bomb scare. I'm a bit worried about being arrested, though.

I have another thought. I call up admissions and say to the woman that answers,

"Hello I'm the personal secretary to His Royal Highness Prince Andrew and he's expressed a very serious interest in coming to your university as a mature student doing English and history. Where do we go from here?"

This is a brilliant plan. I'll get them all excited about him coming, I'll arrange an interview for him and they'll be giddy and laying on a big spread *but* he won't come because I've made it up!

A bored-sounding voice replies, "And when would he be starting?"

"This September," I tell her.

"I think admissions have closed. Let me check."

I'm on hold. She comes back to tell me that they don't do a joint degree of English and history. She goes on to list all the things you can do with English. I pick out English and creative writing. Andrew could always ask Fergie to help him with his coursework.

"Okay," the woman says, "I'll just check that's still open."

I wait a bit and then she tells me it's not; admissions to this course are closed. It's May. The course doesn't start for five months. It's not like I'm calling the night before. And this is for the Queen's son.

I point this out. "Well, as I said before, this is for Prince Andrew." I put a lot of emphasis on the words "Prince" and "Andrew".

"It doesn't work like that," she says.

I'm very surprised. And I feel less bad about them rejecting me all those years ago. Then I tell her that he'll come next year, then. She starts saying he'll have to fill in an UCAS form. Then asks, "What qualifications has he got?"

"Well, he's definitely got a helicopter pilot's licence," I tell her.

There's a long pause. Then she says he'll need to do an access to further education course.

"As I said before, this is Prince Andrew we're talking about," I reiterate.

"It doesn't work like that," I'm told again.

I'm now starting to forget why I'm doing this and become very focused on trying to get Prince Andrew a place at Warwick University.

"What about if there was a significant donation, and I'm talking millions?"

She tells me that they treat everyone the same and it's not her place to talk money. She still sounds so bored. Someone is trying bribery to get a major royal a place at university and I can't help but feel that she's half-listening while thinking about what she'll have for her tea later.

I remember why I'm doing this and give it one more try, "How about he comes down tomorrow and has lunch with you and a look around?"

"He'll only be seen if he has an offer, which he doesn't at the moment, and then he'd have to come down to an Open Day, which actually we have this Saturday."

Big mistake mentioning that.

"Great," I say, "Perfect! What time should he arrive?"

She sighs and says she'll put me through to another department. I'm on hold for so long I get bored and hang up. I've got a feeling this was their intention. Still, I definitely wasted their time a bit, so this was a truly great revenge.

I know who I want to tackle next. Lord Alan Sugar.

I joined Twitter nine months ago and since then I've sent 880 tweets. I'd estimate that around 60% of those have been to Lord Sugar. They are very nice tweets, admiring his work on *The Apprentice* and telling him how much I love his tiny fork diet and like to think of his big fat sausage fingers clasping a tiny fork. Just this week I warned him that I'd seen Tom's nail file, which he invested in on *The Apprentice*, in a bargain bin in a pharmacy in South Woodford. I was doing him a big favour.

All these nice tweets and I've never once got a reply. Yet he's happy to tweet back and forth with the likes of Piers Morgan and Tulisa, and also retweet compliments he gets about his books or his YouView service, for example.

I take it very personally that he consistently ignores me. Now is the time to right that terrible wrong.

I need to get hold of him or someone who regularly speaks to him. I ring up his company Amscreen. I'm afraid that my American accent, once again, has to be used. A woman answers.

"Hi, I'm calling from the United States. I'm from *Time* magazine. You've heard of that, right?"

She has. *Time* magazine, of course, is famous for its Person of the Year, previously won by Barack Obama, Mark Zuckerberg, Pope John Paul II and Gorbachev. But they've not yet announced this year's winner.

I go on with, "I'm calling on behalf of the editor Richard Stengel with some pretty good news for Lord Sugar, so I was hoping to get hold of him."

The woman says that it's best if I contact his PR company as, "We don't see too much of him around here."

Scandalous! He's the chairman!

I call his PR company. I go through the same introduction, the pretty good news and then dive straight in with, "And I'm pleased to tell you we'd love him to be *Time* magazine's Person of the Year."

"That's fantastic," the lady says.

"Yes. As you'll know we choose the person who's done the most to influence events of the year. Obviously, Lord Sugar has done a lot for fledgling businesses with *The Apprentice* and there's the launch of YouView . . ."

She's making encouraging noises.

"And there's that nail file he brought out with Tom."

She goes quiet now.

I fill the silence with a query on how you say the surname of nail-file Tom. I feel like I've got her back again as she asks if it's an interview that we're after.

I tell her, "No just the go-ahead. Obviously, we'd only name someone Person of the Year if we had their permission first."

She asks for my email address. I give her the entirely made up angela.cartwright@timemagazine.com.

She tells me she'll check it's okay with Lord Sugar and then email me back. Of course I won't get this email, but I do get the satisfaction of Lord Sugar thinking for some of today that he is going to be *Time* magazine's Person of the Year.

I'm really enjoying revenge now and I want to seek retribution one more time. It's the boy who said I couldn't sing in 1986.

From the age of ten until sixteen I went to a drama group, Focus Theatre Workshop in Southend-on-Sea. We had an annual production and I memorably starred in *Oliver!* as a workhouse boy, and in *Bugsy Malone* as a boxer, a down and out and Joe the Barman. Three whole parts! I was practically like Eddie Murphy in *The Nutty Professor*. Also, in *Annie*, I was one of the orphans, Pepper. I had one line of singing in "It's a Hard Knock Life", but it was taken away from me, due to the fact that I can't sing.

However, in my first play, when I was about eleven, I

actually had a good part. It was *Sleeping Beauty* and I played Morpheus the Sprite of Sleep. I know it doesn't sound like a great part. I'm not sure it made it into the original story or film, but I did have to do a whole song and dance on my own. It was Paul McCartney's "Frog Chorus". Looking back, I have no idea why Morpheus the Sprite of Sleep sang the "Frog Chorus" and what it has to do with *Sleeping Beauty*. It does feel a little shoehorned in.

Anyway, it was my first role and it was a big one. I felt like there were a few mutterings among my peers about me getting a singing part, but I ignored it and threw myself into the role. I performed my heart out and I thought it went well. Until I saw the VHS recording of one of the performances. During my rendition of the "Frog Chorus", you can very clearly hear a young boy in the audience say in a loud stage whisper, "She can't sing."

The humiliation. I think this was a turning point in my life. I lost my confidence with my singing. I might've become a rich pop star, maybe then an *X Factor* judge. I'd probably be living in that house in Dubai that Nicole Scherzinger once stayed in during judges' houses week.

This young boy wronged me and I will have my revenge.

I know that it's not going to be easy. My first thought is to give the VHS to M15 to use some kind of voice-recognition software on the boy. But I quickly realise this is ridiculous. I've no idea where the VHS is.

I consider ringing up Focus Theatre Workshop to see if they have detailed audience records from a pantomime twenty-six years ago. But it's closed down.

I think to myself, okay, this boy was from Southend so he may well still live there. That narrows it down. I know that he must have some kind of interest in the theatre. (I'm overlooking the fact his parents probably made him go.) And I also know that he's outspoken and confident enough to say this cruel thing about me loudly.

All this points to someone who could now very possibly be active in the Southend am-dram community.

I look for an am-dram society in the area and find Starlight productions. They've got a website and their tagline is, "Where everyone's a star". There's no telephone number, but there is an email address so I send this message:

Dear Sir/Madam,

I wonder if you could help. In 1986 I starred as Morpheus the Sprite of Sleep in a Focus Theatre Workshop production of *Sleeping Beauty*. During my performance I sang the "Frog Chorus" by Paul McCartney. When watching back the video, you could quite clearly hear a young boy in the audience say in a stage whisper, "She can't sing."

I imagine that today he would be between thirty-two and thirty-five and quite possibly still with an interest in amateur dramatics. It is also likely that he has remained opinionated and rude. Is there anybody like that at Starlight Productions as I'd dearly like to get in contact with him.

Please do let me know.

Many thanks and all best wishes,

Annabel

I hear back two hours later. The lady says she will ask if any of the members remember this incident. Then she adds: *And I'm sure you can sing – must've been jealousy.*

I recall their tagline, "Where everyone's a star". This woman has clearly never heard me sing, but I feel I'm getting closer to identifying this boy. When I do, I'm going to find out what he does for a living. Then if he's, say, a car salesman, I'll go to his forecourt and follow him around while he's with customers and say in a loud stage whisper, "You can't sell cars."

This may take some time but I'm setting myself a ten-year deadline. When that person said that revenge is a dish best served cold, I just hope they meant as cold as thirty-six years.

15

The Challenge:
To become a brand ambassador

The golfer Rory McIlroy is being paid £150 million to become a brand ambassador for Nike. £150 million. It's not even like it's a job where he's got to turn up every day.

"That's nice work if you can get it," says Geoff. "So why don't you see if you can get it? Why don't you become a brand ambassador?"

Being a brand ambassador means that you embody the brand's image in appearance, demeanour, values and ethics. I know this because of Wikipedia. What I don't need Wikipedia to tell me is that it's always a celebrity. But this could be a world first, a nobody brand ambassador. I could be good at it. You just need to be loyal to the brand, and I'm someone who's been to Pret A Manger every weekday lunchtime for the last twelve years, including the week when we did the radio show from New York. I'm good at loyalty. And perhaps not too adventurous with food.

To give myself an easy start, I decide to choose a company that has already invested in having a brand ambassador. Then I just need to find a way to replace them.

I look at who's getting all these brand-ambassador jobs. George Clooney's name seems to come up a bit. One of his brands is Omega watches. How hard can this job be, wearing a watch? I've not worn one since I was a teenager so I haven't got any watch fatigue. I'd be a very fresh watch-wearer.

I look more closely into Clooney's involvement and it turns out Omega have several brand ambassadors: Nicole Kidman, Daniel Craig, Cindy Crawford, Ellen MacArthur, Buzz Aldrin and Vanessa Mae.

That is a lot of celebrities to keep track of. I call the marketing department and tell the woman who answers that I have some important information. She tells me that most of the team are out at an event this evening.

It's three o'clock! Their evenings start early. I'm even more surprised when she carries on by saying that they won't be back in the office until Thursday. It's Tuesday! This is the number-one party office in the UK. I want to work there. If I were around fifteen years younger.

The lady says that she might be able to help me.

I say, "The thing is, I saw George Clooney and Cindy Crawford wearing Swatch watches even though they are Omega ambassadors."

"Yes?" she says.

She sounds very interested. But let's bear in mind how bored she must be, stuck alone in the office while everyone else is on some hedonistic forty-eight-hour bender.

I add a bit more detail. "Yeah and they were those Swatch watches with the interchangeable rims around the faces."

I wanted those so much when I was ten. I have no idea if they still exist.

"Where did you see this?" she asks me.

"In London."

She wants more information. "Where in London?"

My brain tries to think of somewhere George Clooney and Cindy Crawford might be in London.

"Near the Dorchester Hotel."

"What, on an advertising hoarding?" she asks.

"No, actually on them. I saw them in real life."

"Oh!" she exclaims. "The actual people."

"And with interchangeable rims on the watch face," I emphasise.

She seems very interested in this detail. Much more so than the detail that I saw George Clooney and Cindy Crawford together.

She says, "I'm not aware of interchangeable rims. I'll talk to the Swatch manager."

I realise now I've made a slight error. Swatch appear to be part of the same company and it looks a lot like they probably stopped doing the interchangeable rings sometime around 1986.

But it's not bothering her. "And sorry, why are you asking? Did you want to buy them?"

She's not yet grasped the full implication. I spell it out for her.

"No, I just wanted to make you aware that George Clooney and Cindy Crawford were wearing non-Omega watches, which seems really bad, considering how much you're paying them."

"Interesting," she says, almost to herself.

Now's my big chance. "And I just wanted you to know that

I'm available to become an ambassador when you get rid of those two."

This is it, surely. Here we go. I start limbering up my wrist for some serious watch-wearing.

"Well, most are high-profile people," she says. "We do have some friends of the brand, like some of the Olympic team, but we don't normally have consumers."

"Don't normally". "Normally". This deal is as good as done.

She tells me she's going to follow it all up with the marketing manager, then adds, "And thank you very much for letting them know about George Clooney and, erm . . ."

There's a pause. I tell her Cindy Crawford. I have concerns that she hasn't written all this information down but she does take my email address. I've pretty much got my first brand-ambassador job.

Just one job is not enough though. Where would George Clooney be if he'd just settled for Omega? Not everywhere holding a Nespresso, for a start.

I need to find a company that can't say no to me as it's just so obvious how much I embody the brand. It's hard to know what would be a good fit for me though. I turn to a friend for help.

"If I were a company, what company would it be?"

"Definitely not a charity," she says immediately. Without any thought. Then she goes quiet for a long time. This appears to be an extremely difficult question. Eventually she says, "Not anything to do with the environment, nothing technological, definitely not a car." There's another long silence.

If you ever want to know what your friends really think about you, this is a good question to ask. I don't recommend it.

After a long time she says, "Maybe a bookshop. You like books. What about Borders?"

I tell her Borders has closed down. There's a pause where I consider that might be her point.

"Well, I don't know then," she says.

This has given me an idea though. It's been in the news that video rental store Blockbuster has gone into administration. Surely other retailers are suffering the effects of Internet sales. Like the bookshop Waterstones. It's like Borders, but open. And I do like reading. It's clear that they need me urgently.

I call up head office. I worry briefly that they'll be on a two-day bender but then figure they're probably too bookish for that. I'm right. I get put through to a stressed-sounding man in marketing. I reassure myself that I'm not wasting his time, I'm saving his job. I say to him, "I'm really worried about Waterstones. Have you considered getting a brand ambassador to save it?"

"Now is not a good time," he says. "I'm in a meeting. Can you call me back in an hour and a half?"

It's a bit weird that he's answering his phone, his desk land-line, during a meeting. It almost feels like a lie. And it almost feels like he's asked me to call back when he knows he'll have gone home.

It just makes me worry about Waterstones even more. So instead of calling back, I send him a lovely email.

Dear Jon,

I'm very concerned about the future of Waterstones as it seems the British high street is currently melting into a pool of liquidised shops.

I have a suggestion. What about getting yourself a

brand ambassador? I understand you've probably sorted out your marketing budget for this year, but I think it would only need a small re-jiggle to put aside money for the ambassador's wages. Perhaps you could close one store. There's a lot in London, two on Oxford Street, in fact, so maybe get rid of one of those. Preferably the one closer to the Marble Arch end as the other one is nearer my work.

You are probably wondering now who this brand ambassador should be. Well, I have a suggestion. What about me? I love books. I read on the Tube and most nights before bedtime. I really enjoy browsing in Waterstones before buying the book I want cheaper on Amazon. I'm perfect.

Here are my ideas as to how I could do this job:

Always have a Waterstones carrier bag on me. Maybe several of them. Filled up with all my stuff.

Tweet about how good the shop is.

Put a sticker on all my books saying "bought in Waterstones". This would work well in spreading the word when I'm reading on the Tube, less so when I'm in bed.

When I buy books on Amazon, I'll do it under a false name so no one knows.

These are just some initial thoughts. Once I've got the go-ahead and we've agreed a fee, I can give you loads more.

Well, I hope to hear from you soon.

Many thanks and all best wishes,

Annabel

I wait to hear back. And I do! Not in the conventional replying to an email way. He's far too busy for that. He lets me know by following me on Twitter. This is clearly the nod, his way of telling me I've got the go-ahead.

I won't bother him any more as I get a tip-off that one of the Waterstones on Oxford Street has a very active Twitter account. It says on the little blurb that it's done by someone called Jonathan.

I tweet them: *I'm your new brand ambassador (unofficial). What do you want me to do?*

I get a reply quickly: *Find the Sword of Rakaka, slay the Hod Clan.*

How exciting! I reply straight away: *I'll do it!*

I've no idea what he means but I'm guessing it's some kind of test and probably all brand ambassadors have to go through this. I wouldn't be surprised if George Clooney only got the Nespresso gig after some similar challenge.

The best place to start is the source of the quest, Waterstones on Oxford Street. I scout around for someone who looks like a Jonathan. I see a man on the shop floor who could be a likely candidate. I sidle up to him with a knowing look and say, "Excuse me, I'm looking for the Sword of Rakaka."

He says, "Okay, I'll just find that for you."

This is so exciting.

He goes behind the till to the book search computer. He's typing in "Sword of Rakaka". He thinks it's a book. Perhaps it is a book. Perhaps it's a book and when I open it, it's got my million-pound ambassador contract inside.

The man is saying now, "Oh right, oh no. No, I can't find it."

He lets me go behind the till so I can see and asks me who

the author is. I show him the tweet from Waterstones but this doesn't seem to clarify the situation in any way. He appears to be very confused. He still wants to help though so he searches for "slay hod" and "hod clan" but finds nothing.

I say, "Maybe it's not a book but an actual sword."

I'd say that he now goes from 0% scared of me to 11% scared of me.

"What, like a toy?" he asks.

"No, a real one," I say. "You couldn't slay hods with a toy. Or a book, come to think of it."

He reluctantly agrees.

I need the help of the official tweeter. I need Jonathan. I ask if he's there. It turns out he's at the other store on Oxford Street.

"Okay I'll go there," I tell him.

He seems very relieved.

I find Jonathan shelf stacking.

"Hi, I'm looking for the Sword of Rakaka."

"Oh," he says, "I spoke to you before."

There's something in his tone of voice that suggests he hadn't expected me to come in.

He's now forced to confess that the Sword of Rakaka is made up. Undeterred, I ask him what I can do instead.

He seems a bit flummoxed by this, so I make a few suggestions.

"What about if I stand outside and encourage people to come in?"

He thinks that this sounds like hassling people. I have another idea. "What if I pick up a book in front of someone and make faces and noises like it's the greatest thing I've ever read? Then they might want to buy it."

"Well, I suppose that would be okay," he says with a hint of reluctance, which I choose to ignore.

There's a lady browsing cookery books. I pick one up.

"Oh wow, oh my God, so interesting!" My enthusiasm is unmistakable.

I see out of the corner of my eye that she's looked up. I keep going. "Noo! Wow. Incredible! Fascinating."

She moves away.

There's a man looking at "Smart Thinking" books. I pick up *Blink* by Malcolm Gladwell.

"Ooh! Oh so great. Ooooh! Yesss! What a book!"

Then I put it back and wait. The man goes to pick up a book. It's not *Blink* though. It's called *The Wisdom of Psychopaths*. I move away.

Jonathan comes over now. "How's it going?"

"Great!" I lie. "Can I have a present for my hard work?"

"Erm, what about a biro?" he says, taking one from behind the till. It's a blue one and I prefer black but I don't make a fuss. I have an image to maintain. I've done it: I'm a paid brand ambassador.

16

The Challenge:
To re-enact a TV show

Geoff has started watching a TV show called *Sing Date*. He says it's better than *Breaking Bad*, *The Sopranos* and *Game of Thrones*. I think he's joking. It's a dating show where a single person picks from three videos of people singing karaoke-style into a webcam. They then meet in the *Sing Date* studio and sing a ballad together. It's very weird.

We watch it together one evening and I make the mistake of saying that I'd love to go on it. Geoff has the next best thing: this challenge.

He wants me to re-enact three TV shows, like you do when you're a kid. When you're a kid you're always pretending to be on your favourite show, like make-believing you are Doctor Who. Me, my sister and our friend Helen were always doing *TJ Hooker*. It's loads of fun. Why don't we do this in adult life? I'm probably about to answer this question in a way that means no one will ever do this in adult life again.

Geoff is very insistent that I start with *Sing Date*. The thought of singing a duet with a stranger, sober and in real life, makes me wonder whether it wouldn't be less humiliating to recreate the dating show *Take Me Out* instead. Even though that would mean thirty tipsy men buzzing their light out straight away, as I'm thirty-seven and haven't got big boobs.

But I get on with it and start by picking the duet. This is the easy bit. It has to be "You're the One that I Want" from *Grease*. There is no better duet.

I download the karaoke version on to my phone. Then I realise I probably need the lyrics for my partner in case they don't know it as well as me. (The relationship will never last if they don't, though.)

I rip a bit of paper out of my Pukka Pad to write them on, but I need to indicate the two different voices somehow and I only have a black biro. I contemplate for a short time writing the Olivia Newton-John part in black biro and the John Travolta part in blood. Just so the difference is clearly seen. But then luckily I remember I've got a pencil tucked into my sudoku book.

I'm ready. The best place to go is where people definitely like singing: a karaoke bar. I'm worried I won't find one that's open during the day, as who does karaoke in daylight hours? But remarkably there is one that's open in Soho from 12 p.m. every day.

I arrive there at about three. There's a man just inside the door. This is great. People *do* go to karaoke during the working day. It turns out he works there, but that doesn't stop me thrusting the lyrics under his nose and playing the backing music out of my phone.

He protests quite a lot. So I try the man behind the till. He says he can't sing unless he's drunk. I'm not sure either have made the right career choices. I give up as I've got a better idea.

When I was going into the karaoke bar I noticed some building work going on a few doors down. I know builders like singing as I remember that advert for Birds Eye Steakhouse grills, where some builders are singing in the back of a van.

"Will it be mushrooms, fried onion rings? We'll have to wait and see," is going round my head as I go up to them. The four of them are all standing in a skip. I'm not really sure why.

I try them all and none want to sing with me, but they point out a guy in a pink top, who's doing some painting, and say that he likes singing.

And he does! He agrees to duet with me. I press play and we get going. His singing is not the greatest, but what I like is that he adds some nice improvised spoken bits to the end of my lines, which include "I'm listening" and "I understand".

This more than makes up for his reluctance to make eye contact with me. I really try but he is very focused on the words.

It goes really well though. I feel we make a real connection. When we finish, my instinct is to hug him, but I hold back as he has quite a lot of inexplicable sweat on his face.

When I go, he tells me he'll be in the same place tomorrow. It's a tentative second date! And as I walk down the road, I can hear all the builders singing the chorus of the song.

It's time for my second show. As well as re-enacting *TJ Hooker*, me, my sister and Helen would also pretend we were in *Fame*, the American drama set in the New York school of performing arts. This show was amazing, so why wouldn't re-enacting it be just as amazing?

I briefly consider flying out to New York but then I remember the recent hurricane. That's definitely the only thing that stopped me and not that I'm reluctant to travel more than ten minutes from my home or work.

I decide to go somewhere more London-based and find a drama school nearby. I'm getting very excited about who I'm going to be. I always wanted to be Coco but I think I've always known that I'm more of a Doris.

When I get there, I go straight up to two women chatting outside.

"Hey!" I say, pointing at a parked car. "Do you want to dance on that with me?"

They were always dancing on parked cars in *Fame* and I have always wanted to do it.

The two women are surprised though. One of them replies, "Well, as delightful as that sounds, I think I'll pass."

The other asks, "But what if you damage it?"

It's a good point. Why did nobody say that in *Fame*? I decide to leave that. Especially as it's a bit cold and I want to go inside, where maybe I'll find the cranky music teacher Mr Shorofsky.

I go to the reception of the drama school. There's an older lady and a younger man in his twenties.

"Hello. I'm here to see Mr Shorofsky," I say to the older lady.

She looks confused. I have to repeat the name. She tells me she doesn't think there's anyone there of that name. I assure her there is. I get told to take a seat.

I hear her asking the other receptionist about a Mr Shorofksy and then on the phone saying his name. I'm still waiting. To pass the time I sing "Starmaker" figuring that all the many people that are passing through will join in. They don't. It's very disappointing.

Eventually I go back to the reception desk to ask if she's found him yet. She still claims not to know who he is.

"It's just that I'm a pianist," I say, "and I was practising a few days ago and Mr Shorofsky overheard me and heard something very special in my playing and told me to meet him here for private lessons."

She's looking at me blankly.

"Shall I show you a picture?" I add.

I've already got one on my phone from Google Images. It's a very standard *Fame* one, the one with him sitting at a piano.

She shakes her head at it. "No, I don't recognise him."

I show it to the younger man. Also nothing. And then the girl standing next to me at reception takes the briefest glance and says in an American accent, "He's a character from *Fame*."

I feign confusion. "Oh, but he works here as well?"

"No, he's in *Fame*," she says. "It's a TV show."

"So he doesn't work here?"

"No, he's a character. Mr Shorofsky is a character. I heard you talking about him, he's a TV-show character."

I look really upset. It's not hard. I've just been caught out asking to see a TV character. The receptionist will probably spend the rest of her days wondering why on earth anybody would do this.

"Oh, so it must be a trick," I say weakly.

"That's so mean," the girl says.

I don't remember this scenario ever featuring in *Fame*, so I have to think for myself what would happen next. I leave.

It's not gone very well compared to *Sing Date* so I move on to Geoff's one other suggestion: The nineties sitcom, *The Brittas Empire*. I loved this TV show. But it's one of those shows like *Sorry* with Ronnie Corbett that I'm too scared to watch again as I strongly fear they are actually terrible.

I have a quick look on the Internet as a refresher. I'm impressed to see that it ran for seven series. And also that it's been described as a "critique of the managerial class which expanded in the Thatcherite eighties".

It's all coming back to me now. There's Gordon Brittas, the manager of the leisure centre, who I like to think was a big inspiration for David Brent. Carol, the receptionist, who kept three children in her reception drawers. I watched the first ten minutes of the first episode. In that short time period they dealt with her postnatal depression. It's grittier stuff than I remember.

I also look at some episode summaries on Wikipedia and all my fears about it not actually being any good disappear. Here are three of my favourites:

> The centre is preparing for a concert by Vladimir Petrov, a visiting pianist from the Leningrad Conservatory. Brittas's father arrives with an old piano, which after being dropped knocks the pianist unconscious. As a result, Gordon decides to perform the concert himself.

> One of Brittas's enemies is coating random items with glue, and shady characters keep appearing. This leads to

a bloody massacre in the squash courts, the felling of several OAPs and Brittas facing trial for multiple murder and drug-running.

TV series *Songs of Praise* visits the leisure centre for a live recording. But a live ostrich is loose, roaming the centre. Meanwhile, Councillor Drugget is still intent on getting rid of Brittas.

Tell me now this wasn't the greatest show ever. I'm very excited about re-enacting *The Brittas Empire* and very inspired reading these summaries. I head off to the leisure centre round the corner from work.

I get into character straight away. I go to reception and say loudly, "Hello, Carol." Even though the receptionist's name badge clearly says Rebekah. She lets it pass.

I carry on with, "I'm Councillor Drugget and I'm here to see the manager about *Songs of Praise* being filmed here today."

She looks a bit bewildered then picks up the phone. "Thanks, Carol," I say.

I hear her saying, "I've got Councillor Drugget here about *Songs of Praise* being filmed here."

There's a pause and Carol/Rebekah asks me who I've spoken to.

"Gordon," I reply.

I'm told there are no Gordons here. I assure her I spoke to the manager, Gordon. There's more discussion on the phone, then I'm told Ben is coming down.

I don't have to wait long. Ben comes towards me, hand outstretched.

"Hello, Gordon," I say shaking his hand.

"It's Ben," he tells me. He's a bit more precious about names than Carol/Rebekah. I introduce myself as Councillor Drugget and explain the *Songs of Praise* situation.

He asks me to go round the corner to a more private area, where he tells me they're not filming here today, he knows nothing about it and he goes on to say why it's not possible. It's boring stuff about health and safety forms and insurance.

I wait for him to finish then say, "Oh Gordon, this is a farce, isn't it?"

He does his best to agree. He's also given up telling me his name is Ben.

"How's everything else?" I ask. "Anything ridiculous happened?"

I'd say he is getting a tiny bit suspicious of me now. He tells me no and leads me back round to reception, where I say, "Carol, I can hear a baby crying – can you? Have you got a baby there?"

Carol/Rebekah looks very confused.

"Gordon, can you hear a baby?"

Gordon/Ben says to me, "Could you just come here again?"

He takes me round the corner to the private area again.

"Are you really from the council?" he asks quietly.

"Yes," I assure him confidently.

He asks if I have any ID. "I'm definitely Councillor Drugget," I tell him.

It's getting awkward now so I say I'm going to make a call about this *Songs of Praise* business to distract him from the fact I'm clearly not from the council.

"Just stay there," he tells me, pointing to a chair, and he disappears.

I'm quite scared. Right now, the very worst-case scenario is not being arrested for impersonating a councillor. It's having to admit I'm an adult playing a game by myself where I'm re-enacting the nineties sitcom, *The Brittas Empire*. And then I realise there is something worse. Admitting I'm doing this for work, for a job. When I could be being a nurse or charity worker or human-rights lawyer. I'm so ashamed. I can't face this.

I pretend to be on my mobile and slowly start backing out of the leisure centre while saying, "Sorry, I can't hear you, the reception's bad, yes, *Songs of Praise*, what's that, hold on, still can't hear, I'm going outside."

Then I leg it. With the knowledge that I have achieved one thing. I really have answered the question of why adults don't re-enact TV shows in real life.

17

The Challenge:
To stage some kind of reunion

Pulp have reunited after nine years. If Pulp can reunite, Geoff reasons, why can't I get back together again with some people? My answer is there's always a reason why you've not seen someone for a while. But this answer is ignored. I have to stage a reunion.

Like the members of Pulp, I've been in bands. Several bands that have long since broken up. My first was called SAS, named after the members: Sarah, Annabel and Sarah. We were eight or nine years old. We had no instruments so were less of a band, more of an a cappella group, but we did write a song called "At the Disco Party Tonight", which we recorded onto cassette in my bathroom.

Then there was Medieval Kyriai when I was eleven. I'd moved on from no instruments to a band with one acoustic guitar. We wrote a song called "Kill Sir Henry". I don't know who Sir Henry was or why we wanted to kill him.

Finally, at fourteen, there was Primrose Path. There was still just one instrument and we did covers of Bangles songs, which I'm sure sounded great with just the drums my friend Michelle was learning to play.

I'm still in contact with the members of the last two bands, so that leaves SAS. It's been twenty-seven years since this band split. I'm worried the reunion will mostly be, "Sorry, who are you?"

I have to find the two Sarahs. I start with Sarah La Plain. I can't find her on Facebook, which is not a good start. But we did go to school together so I do something I've not done in a very long time. It's something that I don't think anyone has done in a very long time. I go on to Friends Reunited. I've not used it for so long that I don't even have the same email address to log on with. I try to do an account retrieval with my new email address and get a message saying it will take twenty-four hours, and even longer at peak times. Really? I'm not convinced they've had a peak time since 2001. So I register again. It's probably the first new registration in at least six years.

I'm in. I find Sarah La Plain and learn that she's changed her surname and also that she works at HSBC.

With her new name, I go straight back to Facebook. I can't find her. I google her name and HSBC and it seems she's a commercial manager at this bank. One phone call to HSBC later, I've found out she works at a branch right by where I work and I have her email address. Being a stalker is easy! Although I suppose the time-consuming bit is sticking up all those photos of your victim on your wall. I don't do that. I send this:

Dear Sarah,

I was wondering if you used to be Sarah La Plain. If so, I believe we went to school together. I'm trying to track down some people for a reunion. Do you remember being in a band called SAS with me and Sarah Lewis? We recorded our single "At the Disco Party Tonight" in my family bathroom.

I try and find the other Sarah now. Sarah Lewis. This is much harder as she's not on Friends Reunited and there are a lot of people called Sarah Lewis on Facebook. I try sending a message to one who has a profile picture of a horse as I seem to remember she liked horses, but I don't hear anything back.

I hear back from Sarah La Plain! It's twenty-four hours after I first wrote, but I ignore the possibility of some reluctance to get back in touch and instead reassure myself that this is still quicker than a Friends Reunited password reset. She writes:

Hi Annabel

Yes it is me!!! Although not sure I remember recording a single in your bathroom!

How are you and how did you track me down? Who else have you got in touch with?

I'm a little hurt that she doesn't remember recording a single in my bathroom. Who doesn't remember their first band? That's like Paul McCartney not remembering the Quarrymen.

There's also not any indication in her email that she remembers me at all and "how did you track me down" suggests a little that she hadn't wanted to be found. But maybe

I'm being paranoid. I push those thoughts aside and press reply.

> Hello! I'm so glad I found you. I can't believe you don't remember SAS and recording "At the Disco Party Tonight"! It was a great song! I'm also trying to get hold of Sarah Lewis. Do you have any idea where she might be?

As you can see, I still haven't mentioned the actual reunion. I don't want to scare her off.

While I wait for a response, I'm thinking, *What's the point of a band reunion without a gig?* We formed when I was eight or nine, so we were an eighties band and these are really popular at the moment. There are lots of reunion tours. In fact, there's a Here and Now tour coming up, featuring Boy George, Midge Ure, Belinda Carlisle, Pepsi & Shirlie, Jimmy Somerville and Flock of Seagulls.

It's being run by Tony Denton Promotions, which seems to do all the eighties reunion gigs and tours. I need to go there and get SAS signed up. I see they're in London. Great. Then I see they're in N14. I look it up and it's zone 4 in north London. A really long way away.

I'd have to travel through five Tube zones to get there. But I'm dedicated to the reunion of SAS, so I make the journey.

I arrive at an anonymous-looking building and press the buzzer. After a while a man answers.

"Hi, I'm here to see Tony. It's Annabel."

He lets me in. I go up the stairs to the second floor and the man has come out of the office to meet me.

He says, "Did you have a meeting booked? Tony's not actually here."

I'm very disappointed. "Oh, I'm here about the Here and Now tour. Is there anyone else that can help?"

"No, there's nobody else here. Just me."

I'm not giving up.

"It's just that I'm from an eighties band."

"Oh, right." He doesn't seem very interested. This just makes me more persistent.

"Don't you recognise me?"

He looks a bit embarrassed and says, "No."

"Take a guess, go on."

"I wouldn't like to."

I give him a clue. "It was the early eighties."

I'm kind of hoping at this point that he says, "But you don't look old enough to have been in a band in the early eighties."

He doesn't. He just says, "Sorry, I really don't know."

It's getting a bit awkward so I say, "SAS!"

"Oh."

The situation isn't any less awkward.

I add, "Sarah, Annabel, Sarah."

"No." He can't even be bothered to pretend.

"'At the Disco Party Tonight', our one-hit wonder?"

"No, sorry."

I suppose it's good that he didn't know us or that would've meant he'd been peeping into my bathroom at some eight-year-olds twenty-seven years ago. I don't mention this though, as I suddenly see, through their glass door, a man walking past in the distance.

I blurt out, "I've just seen someone. You said no one was here. Is that Tony?"

He's looking very uncomfortable now. He says, "No, he's

out of the country. Not back until four."

He offers to take my details though and goes to get some paper.

"Shall I come?"

"No, you stay here," he says quickly.

He comes back with a pen and notepad.

I take them and then in desperation I give him a blast of "At the Disco Party Tonight". I sing:

> The lights are flashing, the music's loud,
> The people are dancing, it's such a crowd,
> At the disco party tonight,
> Boom, boom, boom,
> At the disco party tonight.

He's looking fairly horrified now. I write down my band name, email address and number and he says Tony will get back to me.

I'm very concerned. I've still not heard from Sarah La Plain and I'm on the verge of signing up SAS for the tour. I think. I email her again. It's time to break the big news.

Hi Sarah,

Just wanted to let you know some great news. I had a meeting yesterday at Tony Denton Promotions about SAS joining the eighties Here and Now tour featuring Boy George and Belinda Carlisle, among others.

I'm speaking to them again today so just wanted to check your availability for this tour. The dates are:

Birmingham 24 June

Liverpool 25 June

Manchester 26 June
Newcastle 29 June
Sheffield 30 June
London July 1
How does this sound? It'll be great to get the old
band back together again. I still need to track down Sarah
Lewis, though. Do you have any contact details for her?

If you don't have time to reply to emails at work,
perhaps I could pop down to your office later on this
afternoon.

Let me know what you think.

Annabel x

I wait for her reply. I'm doing a lot of waiting as I've still not
heard back from Tony Denton Promotions, despite leaving all
my details yesterday. I've no choice but to call them up. I'm
not going across five Tube zones again. Not even for SAS.

The same man I met yesterday answers the phone.

"Hi. Can I speak to Tony, please?"

"Can I ask who's calling?"

"It's Annabel."

There's a very long pause. Then he says, "Hold the line."
I wait.

He returns to say that Tony is on another call at the
moment. I tell him I'll call back in half an hour.

I wait half an hour. Then call back. "Hi, can I speak to Tony?"

"Can I ask who's calling?"

"Annabel."

"Okay."

It's the coldest okay I've ever heard. I'm on hold again.
When the man comes back, he says that Tony has popped out

of the office and he's no idea how long for.

"Did you give him the message?" I ask. He says that he did.

"Did he look excited? Because I'd expect him to be excited."

"I don't know," the man replies.

"Shall I call back in half an hour?"

"I'll get him to call you."

I know how it seems. It seems that Tony is avoiding me. But I think he's trying to juggle the line-up to incorporate SAS without offending Belinda Carlisle or Pepsi & Shirlie, and he doesn't want to speak to me until it's sorted.

So that's all good. But I've still not heard from Sarah and this is my last day, time is running out. I have to email again. I write:

Hi Sarah,
    What do you think of the dates? Shall I pop down to
your office now to discuss?

Still nothing, until an hour later I get an email with an HSBC address from someone called Paul. I can see the first line:

I work with Sarah.

My blood runs cold. I've got an email from one of the main high-street banks warning me to stop harassing their staff. I read on.

We've been having a bit of a laugh about the band
reunion. Sarah thinks it's some kind of wind-up.

The relief! I tell him it's definitely not a wind-up. We email back and forth. He's the international commercial manager of HSBC and he's got involved as a mediator to try and get the band back together again. Maybe this is what happened with Pulp. Maybe the international commercial manager of Barclays sorted it all out.

Paul tells me that Sarah still needs persuading. He's worried as she recently ducked out of the work's karaoke night out. It's not great. I'm nervous that she's got some kind of vocal problem. Throat polyps or something.

SAS will have to become AS. Then I remember that I've got no way of getting hold of Sarah Lewis and realise it will have to become just A.

I sit on my bed and sing to myself:

> *The lights are flashing, the music's loud,*
> *The people are dancing, it's such a crowd,*
> *At the disco party tonight,*
> *Boom, boom, boom,*
> *At the disco party tonight.*

It is a pitiful reunion.

18

The Challenge: To write and publish some erotica

My experience of dirty writing is almost entirely limited to Judy Blume's *Forever*. I read it twenty-four years ago. The fact I call it "dirty writing" says a lot. I need to find out what people want today.

Of course, I have some idea already. They clearly want *Fifty Shades of Grey*. It's currently the fastest-selling paperback of all time. Naturally, I've not read it, so I use Google to give me the gist. I find this:

> It is notable for its explicitly erotic scenes featuring elements of BDSM.

I have to look up BDSM. It sounds like a driving school. I'm guessing it's not. It's not. From what I've read, I'd summarise it as being a bit strict.

While carrying out this important research, something else has caught my eye. A mention of furries.

Surprisingly, I do know about furries. (A friend told me about it. Honestly. I've not done it. This is the truth.) It's a fascination with anthropomorphic animals that can get a bit, what I'd call, seedy. Perhaps this could be the next big thing in erotica? Perhaps this is what women now want?

I devise a survey to find out. I write the word "Survey" at the top of a bit of paper and then the word "Furries" and then a gap.

It looks a bit empty and un-survey-like so I have a really long think for around ten seconds and decide that as people are getting excited about the Olympics at the moment, maybe some erotica based around an Olympic sport might be nice.

I add the words "Olympic sport" to my survey. Then because I want to tap into what people really want, I add: "Other?"

I take my survey onto the streets, to my target audience, the ladies. I say to the first lady I approach, "Hello, I'm an erotic fiction author, could I ask you a few questions?"

She's happy to do this. "Would you like to read some erotica about people into being furries?"

Once I've explained furries, she replies that she would.

"What about an Olympic sport?" I continue.

She would.

I'm feeling really positive. I try another lady. When asked about furries, she's less keen. Quite adamant, in fact, that it wouldn't turn her on.

But when I mention the Olympics, she becomes interested and even suggests gymnastics as a suitable sport. I ask for other suggestions.

"I'd just like something with meaning and depth, some-thing that challenges me," she says.

This is going to be a massive problem. But I lie and say, "Well, that's what I'll do."

The next woman I talk to is outside a pub. She tells me furries is not her cup of tea and that she's not interested in the Olympics. So I press her to tell me what she does like and this complete stranger tells me, "Well, I'm really into bondage and tying up, handcuffs, strangulation."

"What are you strangling with?" I ask.

"Hands," she replies.

I make a mental note to use hands in my book.

I ask one more girl. She isn't mad on any of the ideas and doesn't have any suggestions. But perhaps she wasn't the best person to pick as she was standing outside work with two male colleagues, one of whom, it emerged, was her boss.

However, I feel this is pretty thorough research by my standards, and I now have a great sense of what the ladies want from my erotica. Furries doing gymnastics at the Olympics with a bit of strangulation.

I just need to find out a bit more about furries. The first thing I discover is that they've got their own language.

Yiff means sex. Yiffy is feeling sexual and yiffing is mating. I'm really struggling to find mating a sexy word. And yiffing.

There's one website that appears to be at the centre of all the action. It's called sofurry.com. I definitely need to join it. I'm asked to choose a username. I try AnnabelAnimal. It's free! I log in and go straight to the chat room. But it's terrible news. There's a twenty-four-hour cooling-off period before you can chat. Like at casinos. In case you get carried away and regret it in the morning.

Luckily there is also a forum, which I can post on straight away. I start a new thread.

> Hi Furries – I'm new – want to have some fun? I'm a
> new Furry and feeling yiffy.

I want to say something now about what I look like but I
need inspiration. I go on a website that sells fur animal outfits. I
find myself quite interested in a giraffe as I like the idea of long
eyelashes, long neck and long legs. I consider a penguin but am
put off by the short legs. A kangaroo appeals as I'd be able to
keep tissues in my pouch. A seal is definitely out; this is not in
any way yiffy. I'm seriously considering a flying squirrel when I
see a hamster, which I know immediately is for me.

I'm ready to carry on with my message. I write:

> I'm a new Furry and feeling yiffy. Here's what I look like.
> I look like a hamster. A grey one that can fit all sorts in
> my cheeks. A whole mangetout and a whole floret of
> broccoli. I've got little tender paws that like tapping. And
> a soft tummy. I like going in my wheel, round and round,
> round and round, round and round, round and round.
> Let's have fun together!
> Xx

I regret the kisses after I press "post". I had been planning
on being the Julia Roberts in *Pretty Woman* of the furries
world. But it's too late, as to my surprise, my message goes
straight up, with no moderating. I wait for the responses to
flood in.

In the meantime, I continue my important research by
ringing up the website that sells the furry animal outfits, to
get a feel for what's going on.

A man answers. I don't want to get yiffy straight away in
case it's not his scene and he hangs up. I cleverly start with,

"What is your most popular animal?"

He tells me it's the giraffe. I think that's probably enough filler so I go on with, "And which is the best if you're into the erotic side of things?"

"I don't know, that's not what we do," he says.

This is disappointing. But perhaps he's embarrassed and doesn't want to admit it. So I push on. "But which do you think would be best?"

He goes with wolf.

"And what animal do you think would go with a wolf?"

"I'm not sure anything goes with a wolf. I could do you two cats though."

I'm not keen on this. A bit screechy.

"What do you think would go with a giraffe?" I ask.

He feigns ignorance again. I'm getting frustrated. "Do people not buy the costumes for erotic stuff?"

"No," he says with surprise. "For parties."

He's so naive.

I decide to go back to check on my forum posting. There's a response! From a website ambassador called Beowolf1990. I'm a bit worried about the 1990 thing as this suggests more youth than I feel comfortable with, but I read on.

> Aren't you the most adorable thing? Welcome to the site! If you ever have any specific questions, myself and any of the other ambassadors will be more than happy to help you out. And personally, I am always up for a chat, so never hesitate to shoot me a PM :)

I spend some time worrying if "adorable" is a good thing in the furry world. Until I spot another response. It's from Red Back Dragon. He (I'm guessing it's a he) is keeping it simple with a straightforward:

Hi

I reply immediately.

Hi there! How are we all going to have fun together?
I've got one of those clear balls that hamsters run
around in ...

Nothing back. No response.
I reply to a racoon's greetings with:

My tummy is itchy. Will you scratch it?

Nothing.
A fox has introduced himself with:

Welcome, enjoy your stay. *Passes the bottle of vodka
and a plate of cookies*

I post back:

Well, vodka and cookies are a great start (although
perhaps not advisable for hamsters) – what shall we do
now?!

Nothing.
I start worrying that my hamster isn't very sexy and then
feel horrified that I'm having these thoughts. I decide to call
it a day and then come back tomorrow when my cooling-off
period has expired and I'm able to join the chat room.

It's the next morning and I've cooled off but I'm still keen so
head straight to the chat room. I try and get some stuff going.
To a wolf I write:

Hi wolfie! I'm a hamster – want to tickle my tummy?

I attempt to seduce a fish with:

Hi fish! Want to nibble some fish food out of my
hamster cheeks?

They both ignore me. It's starting to become embarrassing. Until I'm approached by a wolf.

I'd be interested, he huskily whispers. I imagine. I also imagine again that it's a he. This is much more exciting. Especially when he invites me into a private room. And while I don't want anyone to think I'm easy, for the purposes of research, I'm straight there.

This is what happens:

Me: hi there
Wolf: The nude husky stands before you, my athletic
form just over six feet. I lick my maw lips, looking at you.

While I'm trying to decipher "maw", he says something incredibly rude, followed by:

Wolf: You were saying you wanted to get wild?
Me: Yes. Wild. I'm running on my wheel with excitement
and baring my little teeth.
Wolf: Well, why don't you come over and show me how
wild?
Me: I want to bite you – but nicely.
Wolf: That's fine.
Me: I'm biting you now on the nose – how does it feel?
Wolf: More odd than anything.

I'm no expert but I don't think this is a very sexy response.

Me: Okay, how about I gnaw gently on your claws?

I wait. No response. Then the humiliation. The wolf leaves the private room. I'm there alone. Rejected, exposed, vulnerable. I close the browser window. Then delete my Internet history. Then my cookies, even though I don't really know what this means.

But the good thing is, I've learned a lot and now feel ready for the writing and inevitable publishing.

I sit down to write. I'm feeling very inspired by the last twenty minutes of the film *The Human Centipede*, which I caught on the television last night. I'm also confident that I know what women want. Furries at an Olympic setting and some other unsavoury things.

I choose the character names Katherine and Michael. They are both furries. Katherine is a hamster, Michael is a husky dog. The words flow from me. Here is the result. It's called Cheeks.

Cheeks

Katherine stroked the soft fur gently. Then stroked the cool, very thin cardboard of the tickets. She sighed with happiness. Her larynx vibrated with the sigh. Then her phone vibrated as well, as it was ringing.

"Hello," whimpered Katherine.

"Hello," barked Michael.

"I'm five minutes away," he said next. "Have you eaten your seeds and sucked some drops of water from your upturned bottle?"

Katherine stroked the fur again as she replied with, "Yes and I've saved some seeds in my cheeks for later so my cheeks look really big."

Michael didn't answer. Just hung up.

Katherine didn't have much time. She quickly pulled

her hamster suit on. Underneath she had her vest and pants and 120 denier tights as the suit was a bit itchy. She found her left hand skimming her left calf as it went on and she went a bit breathless like an asthmatic struggling to breathe so they don't die.

She pulled up the zip as the doorbell went. She ran downstairs but had to go back as she'd forgotten the tickets.

Katherine opened the door. There was nobody there. Then she heard a "Ruff". She looked down. There was a husky dog on all fours. She did a double take. And then realised it was Michael and he'd had extensive plastic surgery to look like a husky dog. She felt funny in her tummy, in a good way.

"Let's go," Michael barked. "Have you got your plastic ball?"

Katherine nodded.

"Well, get in it, then – I don't want you running away."

Katherine climbed inside the see-through plastic ball and then began crawling so she could move down the high street. Michael scampered alongside her.

Eventually they got to Stratford and Katherine had to get out of the ball to hand the steward the tickets. They were going to watch the 100m final at the 2012 Olympics.

They went to their seats. The race was starting. The men were running really fast. The speed made Michael feel passionate. He pawed at Katherine and nuzzled her. Then he kissed her. Some of her seeds fell on to the floor.

"Scratch my tummy," she commanded. He did it. Then they heard a cheer. Usain Bolt was the winner.

They stood up and had a lovely cuddle. Katherine secretly took a needle and thread from her cheeks and secretly sewed her fur to Michael's husky fur. Katherine's cheeks were now less fat. Michael howled.

The end.

As far as I can see, all I need now is the publishing deal and my challenge is complete.

I head off to a publishing house. I know it's no good turning up saying I've got a book I want publishing. I'm no fool. I know they only deal with agents.

It's clear then that I have to become an agent. Which means I need a name for the author. Something along the lines of *Fifty Shades of Grey's* E. L. James.

My first two initials are A. E. so I decide to start with that and then for the surname toy with: A. E. Clementine, A. E. Scarf, A. E. Bandage, A. E. Hand, A. E. Elbow and A. E. Neck. I finally settle on A. E. Thigh.

I need a name for my agency and decide Eroticabel would be nice. I'm feeling very prepared. I've got a print-out of the first chapter with me. It fits nicely on to one side of A4. I go up to the door and press the buzzer. It opens.

There's a hallway leading round to a room on the left. As I go in, I put my phone up to my ear and say loudly, "No, no, I'm telling you now she will not write another chapter unless we settle on five million."

I'm in the reception now, which looks like a big posh drawing room with a lady at the far end behind a desk. She's looking at me a bit strangely.

"I've got to go," I bark into an unconnected phone.

Then I stride up to the desk and say, "Hi, I'm the well-known agent Annabel Port from Eroticabel. I've got a great new author called A. E. Thigh—"

She interrupts me. "Sorry, who are you here to see?"

She soon ascertains that I don't have an appointment. But I'm not letting that get in the way. "Let's sort this out," I say, in the way that I imagine Lord Alan Sugar might say it.

Her phone is ringing now. She apologises and takes the call.

But maybe I've got a phone call to take too. My phone goes to my ear again and I'm saying, "I'm sorry but it's not up for discussion, it's five million or no chapter."

She's off the phone again and tells me she's just seeing if anyone is around and that I should take a seat. This is unexpected.

I wait for a while and then a man appears. He comes into reception and towards me. He's wearing a checked shirt and jeans and he's slightly posh, very sweet and good looking in a bookish way.

I introduce myself and we sit down on the reception chairs. I dive straight in.

"Let me tell you about my author. With *Fifty Shades of Grey*, erotica is a big thing at the moment."

We then get into a discussion about whether it is going to be a big thing or if it'll just be this book. He doesn't know. He also says they're not doing any erotica at the moment.

"Well, you should," I tell him.

Then as I pull out the first chapter, I add, "Do you know about furries?"

He doesn't.

"Well," I tell him, "It's people who are into dressing up in animal costumes and doing 'you know what' while wearing them."

He laughs awkwardly and glances up at the receptionist with a look that suggests he wishes she hadn't called him down here.

I don't stop though. "And this novel is set to the backdrop of the Olympics and there are other elements." I bottle mentioning *The Human Centipede* as I fear I'm losing him.

"Well, we'd expect to see the whole book," he says. I have forced the chapter into his hands now. He's reading it and looking slightly terrified.

"Katherine is a hamster," I blurt out. "And Michael's a husky dog."

He laughs very awkwardly again. Then asks me if I've got a card. Of course I don't. I'm from an entirely made-up agency. Instead I write my telephone number at the top of the first chapter print-out and tell him I'll get A. E. Thigh to finish the novel.

"Great," he says, then gives me his full name, adding that if I ring reception they'll probably put me straight through. I'm unsure if that was a barbed comment directed at the receptionist.

I leave thinking it went pretty well, but I'm worried about how long it takes to actually produce a book. First, it's got to be written. Then there's the editing process, the cover design, marketing strategy devised, the printing.

I need immediate results so I decide to publish online. And I know exactly where to go. The SoFurry website. Home to all my research. I upload my story. I have to tag it with at least two tags so I use "Yiff" and "Yiffy".

It doesn't go up straightaway. I worry that it needs to be moderated, then worry I did it wrong, so I post it again and both go up at the same time, which is a bit embarrassing.

But it's there, my story, my erotica. Published. Sort of. And by the end of the day there have been nineteen views. Nineteen! Just think how many of these felt yiffy and then did yiffing after reading my story. I feel sick.

19

The Challenge:
To get nominated for an award

We're in the thick of awards season. It was the Brits last night and we've just had the Grammys, BAFTAs and Golden Globes. The Oscars are next.

Geoff says, "What would be lovely for the show, would be if you got yourself nominated for some kind of award."

"Me?"

"Yes."

"Me?"

"Yes."

"I don't mean a radio award or anything," Geoff adds.

"No, obviously not," I say.

The good news is I just have to get nominated, I don't have to win. There is one condition though. I have to be nominated for a pre-existing award. I can't just make one up. That's my first idea ruined. The bad news is he also wants me to get thanked in an awards ceremony speech.

I start by seeing what awards ceremonies are coming up and discover that tonight, it's the RCC Awards. The awards of the Redhill Cycling Club. A club in Surrey with around 400 members who take cycling seriously. It says "for members only", but that doesn't put me off.

The only way to contact them is to email through the website. I write:

Dear Sir/Madam,

I would like to be nominated for an award at your prize-giving ceremony. You fail to list the categories on your website but I can't do wheelies, so don't put me forward for best wheelie. I also find it difficult to indicate that I'm turning left, something to do with not being able to balance with only my right hand on the handlebars. I'm probably not suitable for a maintenance award either as my bike has had a puncture for over two years. Recently, though, I saw a squirrel sitting on the seat like it was about to ride it. So that might help you.

All the best,

Annabel

I'm slightly nervous about ever hearing back so I look to see if any other awards are coming soon and find the perfect one.

The ceremony is two months away in Manchester. It's hosted by BBC *Breakfast*'s Carol Kirkwood. It's the UK Coach Awards. The transport type, not the training-person type. I had no idea this existed. I wonder if anyone's ever won "Having a coach with a working toilet". I imagine not.

I don't own a coach or coach company, but I've been on a coach before. Lots of times. In fact, I've gone by coach to

Poland twice, and that's a twenty-four-hour journey.

I have a look at the categories and the one that stands out for me is the prize for "Unsung Hero". I truly feel like a hero for doing those twenty-four-hour journeys. This is the one.

The nominations come from readers of *Coach & Bus Week* magazine. If I can get to the readers of this magazine, I'm sure I can get nominated. After all, how big can the circulation be? It's not the type of magazine you're going to find in your local newsagent's but there's a place called Ian Allen Bookshops near Waterloo that stocks it.

I write out a series of notes that I'm going to slip into all copies of *Coach & Bus Week*.

It's paper I've ripped out from my notebook. On it I've written:

> **Vote Annabel Port**
> **From Annabel Port Coaches**
> **For the Unsung Hero Award**
> **At the UK COACH AWARDS**

Then I thought I'd better add a reason so I put:

> **As she never gets annoyed in traffic**

I write that a few times then get bored and change it to:

> **As she swerved to save a mouse**

Which after a while gets changed to:

> **As she swerved to save a pig**

I'm at the bookshop now. It's a Mecca for transport enthusiasts. There are books and magazines on trains, buses, aircraft and trams. Trains really dominate. There is lots of model railway stuff. They also sell some toy soldiers. They really know their demographic.

So do I after being in here for less than five minutes. Apart from the woman at the till, I'm the only female in there. Possibly ever.

I go in search of *Coach & Bus Week*. There's a massive problem. While they do have several copies, all but one are sealed in a plastic wrapping, to secure a supplement of *Coach World*.

And the one without plastic wrapping is over a month old. In fact, there's only one copy of the most recent edition.

There's only one thing I can do. I slip one of my notes in the open one and then take the wrapped ones to the till. I say to the lady,

"Can I make a small slit in the plastic and slip this note in?"

This is a shop dedicated to all things transport. This cannot be the strangest thing anyone has ever asked her. But she acts like it is. And it's a no.

But we come to a compromise. She assures me that she will keep the notes by the till and whenever anyone buys a copy of *Coach & Bus Week*, she'll hand them one.

This is great. I'm very optimistic. And something even better has happened. I check my email and find that I've heard back from the chairman of the Redhill Cycling Club regarding their awards:

Hello Annabel,

I'm happy to inform you that you are in the running for the "Best Email" trophy. Should the judges decide that

you will be awarded this prize, we will contact you in
plenty of time to hire an appropriate Gucci dress for the
ceremony.

I'm slightly insulted that he assumes I'm not able to buy a
Gucci dress outright. Even though he's right.

I email straight back telling him I'm thrilled and ask him to
give me confirmation of my nomination as soon as possible.

It's the day after the night before. The night of the Redhill
Cycling Club awards, where I think I was nominated for
"Best Email". Do I need to wait in in case they'd posted me my
trophy? I email the chairman again to ask him how I did on
the big night.

Then I turn my attention back to the UK Coach Awards.
The notes I left in some out-of-date magazines might not be
enough. I'd scoured the unsealed copy of the magazine but
there was no information on how you vote for Unsung Hero.
I find a number for Pat, the award's administrator, and call
her up.

The number goes to answerphone, which informs me
that on Tuesday, Wednesday and Thursday mornings until
1.30 p.m., they're in a meeting.

That is a lot of meeting time. There's now an option to leave
a message or call Pat's mobile number. I choose the latter.
There's no answer. She's probably in another meeting. I leave a
message asking her to call back urgently re: the Unsung Hero
award.

I'm not holding out much hope, what with Pat's heavy
meeting schedule, so I call up *Coach & Bus Week* magazine.

A lady answers. I ask her how, as a reader of *Coach & Bus*

Week magazine, I can vote for Unsung Hero in the UK Coach Awards.

"Let me find out," she says and puts me on hold for around a minute. There's no hold music. I was hoping for "National Express" by Divine Comedy.

When she comes back she says I need to contact Pat at the coach awards. This doesn't seem right to me. Every person ringing Pat to make their nomination. It also sounds logistically impossible as Pat is always in one long meeting.

"Was it not in the magazine?" I ask.

The woman is getting defensive now. "Yes, it's been in a few; we did a double-page spread in one."

"So how did it say to vote when it was in the magazine?"

"The awards are nothing to do with me," she says. Then she puts me on hold again for another minute before coming back to tell me she's found an old copy of the magazine and you vote online at the website, where you can download a form.

I'm feeling now like she wants to get rid of me so I go back on the UK Coach Awards website, but there is nowhere to vote for Unsung Hero. In fact, the shortlists for all the other awards have already been announced. Not for Unsung Hero though. I'm getting worried.

But I'm momentarily distracted from all this by an email from the chairman of Redhill Cycling Club. I click on it. The following message appears:

Hi Annabel

Yes, your email received huge support from the vast audience. There were tears, laughter, screams of joy and anguish when – I'm afraid – you didn't scoop the Cycling

BAFTA equivalent in this hard-fought category.

The email from one of our longest-standing members enquiring about the best spokes to use during the winter months pipped you at the post, I'm afraid.

I know that this will be devastating but I can only encourage you to keep submitting emails at the high standard you have already set.

There's always next year.

With commiserations

Adrian

Chairman

This is clear favouritism towards a long-standing member rather than me, not a member at all. Or never even been to Redhill. Unless you count passing by on a train. But I did get nominated. I think.

And there's still hope that Pat might come out of a meeting and get back to me about the Coach Awards.

I've still not heard back from Pat. I try calling again and the phone is answered by a Pat-sounding woman. But it isn't Pat. It's Margaret. Pat is out of the office until this afternoon.

"Is she in a meeting?" I ask.

"Yes," Margaret says.

While I'm not entirely giving up on the UK Coach Awards, I do feel like I should be maybe looking at a ceremony that is a bit better organised. Something bigger. Like the Oscars this Sunday.

It is too late to be nominated. And I've not been involved in a film in the past year. But, I could get a thank you in an acceptance speech. I hadn't forgotten about this part of the challenge.

I look at the nominations. Colin Firth has one. I'm trying to think if I know him. Then I realise I don't.

Banksy is nominated for best documentary. It might be tricky to get hold of him. Although probably not as tricky as Pat.

I look to see if anyone else British been nominated and I find a man who has been shortlisted for Best Visual Effects in the film *Inception*.

I look him up and his company is on Shaftesbury Avenue in central London. This is great.

I can go there, meet him and then ask him to thank me if he wins the Oscar on Sunday.

There are two cool young guys on reception.

"Hi. I'm here to see Ben Franklin."

"Oh, okay. What's your name?"

I give it to them.

"Is it for an interview?"

"Kind of," I say.

I'm not looking for a new job, but there will be questions and answers.

They take my photo, which is a bit weird, but I give them a lovely smile. Then they tell me to take a seat.

After a short while, one of the guys calls over to me, "I take it he's expecting you?"

"I think I made an appointment but my memory isn't great," I say.

He gives a half laugh. A short while later he asks, "Are you sure it's Ben Franklin? There's no one here of that name. Was it Paul Franklin?"

"Oh," I say. "Is Paul Franklin the top dog, the Oscar man?"

It appears I may have made a slight faux pas. By getting one of the founding fathers of the United States confused with the head honcho at visual-effects company.

I hear them mumbling now about how they don't think he's in today, how he's usually in that office over there. But they say to me that it's being sorted and someone is coming out to see me.

That someone is a woman called Ashley. She introduces herself as the PR manager and says she's a bit confused as she takes me into a meeting room.

"Did you have a meeting set up with Paul?" she asks.

"Well, I might've done but my memory is not great."

She starts really apologising and saying that I've just missed him as he left for the Oscars yesterday and that she didn't know about the interview.

"Is it about the Oscars?" she asks.

It's gradually dawning on me that they don't think I'm here for a job interview. They think I'm here to interview Paul Franklin. Although they've not asked me where I'm from. It's probably time for me to leave.

Ashley asks me to email her and then says she'll get in contact with Paul and try and set something up.

I'm well on my way to getting acknowledged at the Oscars. Should I get to speak to Paul and then Paul agrees to thank a total stranger for no reason at all during the biggest career moment of his life. Oh, and that's if he wins. If not, I'll always have the Best Email nomination at the Redhill Cycling Club awards.

20

The Challenge: To invent a
new kind of clothing

This is finally my big chance to use the skills I learned in GCSE textiles over twenty years ago. Even though, as you may remember, I actually got my mum to do my coursework of making a dress and only got a C, which she was not happy about.

I know it's hard to imagine, looking at me now, but I was very interested in fashion when I was younger. When I was twelve, my friend Tessa and I invented a new trend of wearing tights with shorts, which we debuted at the school disco to much apathy.

I also remember wearing, at another school disco, a gingham puffball skirt hitched up on both sides by mini gingham braces, revealing a petticoat I was wearing underneath. This is the kind of crazy creativity we're dealing with.

I can definitely see a big gap in the clothing market, a

much-neglected area. The face. My face is always cold. And it annoys me that if you have a bad hair day, you can wear a hat. If you have a bad face day, there's nothing you can do. There is the balaclava, but it's a bit terroristy. And a bit woolly. I need something a bit more high fashion. I make a note to come back to this.

I'm thinking now about how the onesie has become a big thing recently and I'm very bitter about that. I was saying for years I wanted an adult babygro, which is what it is, but I never did anything about it. I could be a onesie millionaire right now.

Still, maybe there's more to be mined from the baby world. I very briefly think about adult nappies but realise this would be less of a fashion invention and more a breakdown of society.

I consider bibs for a bit. They'd be good for jazzing up a plain T-shirt and you can just take it off if it gets messy. I also think about booties. They kind of already exist for adults with the boot-like slipper. That's a cross between a bootie and a slipper. Or as I call it, the blipper.

Maybe there are some other hybrids I could create. Like when they did the cross between the jean and the legging, the jegging. In these difficult financial times, I think people want more from clothes.

I have a brainwave. What about an item that from the front is a skirt but from the back, a pair of trousers? I start sketching what this might look like. I'm in a cafe.

A man walks past and says, "Nice drawing!"

"Thanks!" I say and go into great detail about what it actually is. He looks like he deeply regrets saying "nice drawing".

Especially when I really push him to say whether he'd consider wearing the skirt/trouser hybrid.

"In private, maybe," is his answer.

This is real encouragement.

I think I'm going to go with this hybrid and call it the "Skousers". Either that or the face thing. I'll run up a prototype of both and let the people decide.

By a stroke of luck, I've had a bag of old clothes by my front door for the last year that I've been meaning to take to the charity shop but never got round to it.

If that's painting a nice picture of the area by my front door, you've not yet added the months of unopened post and ignored takeaway leaflets, the shoes, the bag of scarves that needs to be sorted out and a knife that I once used to try and open the light fitting outside the front door. That's the complete picture.

I rummage through the bag and find an old denim skirt. There are no trousers but there is a pair of black leggings that had gone very saggy around the bottom area. They will have to do.

I start with the skirt. This only needs to be seen from the front so I just cut most of the back off. Then I get the leggings and cut the entire front of the legs out but leave a small bit around the ankle to stop them flapping. I'm a bit short on time so I don't sew the two together but use safety pins.

The Skousers are ready.

Next, the face mask. I've got some floral material that I fashion into a face covering, with holes cut for the mouth and eyes. And as I've got some spare denim left over from the Skousers, I give it a nice denim trim. Now it's not just functional, it's also stylish. I decide to call it the "Fask".

I take my revolutionary new clothes into work. The receptionist has concerns I look like a more colourful member of the Ku Klux Klan. The head of marketing, Clare, walks past and says I look creepy.

This is not the reaction I was hoping for. But are they fashion experts? Are they the right people to advise me before I pitch my creation at London Fashion Week?

There are lots of boutique shops around Carnaby Street, near our offices. I'll take my creations there to get some feedback and advice. Maybe there are some slight alterations it would be best to make.

I go into a men's clothes shop. The clothes seem quite edgy, so this is perfect.

"Hi. I've got some great designs I'd like to show you," I say to the two men at the till. They both look trendy. I suspect the fact that I'm using the word "trendy" means that I'm not trendy.

I put the mask on first, the Fask.

"Are you going to rob us?" one says, but in a jokey way so I don't think they're pressing the panic button under the counter.

"Oh, does it look a bit robber-y?" I say.

"Are you serious?" they ask. They ask that question a lot over the next few minutes, despite me telling them I am serious. I feel like John McEnroe's umpire.

I move on to the Skousers now. They are very polite about them and smiling a lot.

"Do you think you'd stock these designs?" I ask.

"Oh, you'd have to ask head office."

I can't get much more out of them so I go to a ladies'

boutique with a French name. There's just one lady in there. I show her the Fask.

"Oh no," she says.

"What?"

"It's like a gimp mask."

I get the Skousers out. She's a bit politer about them and says that clubbers might like them.

"Do you want to try them on?" I ask.

"No!" she says, really abruptly.

But that's okay. I've got all the feedback I need for my pitch now.

I've never done a pitch before. Luckily I've seen *The Apprentice* many times so I know all about them. How it's best not to do a collage or to take your shoes off and dance. I also know that you write it in a taxi on the way to the pitch. I can't afford a taxi so I do it on the Tube instead.

London Fashion Week is at Somerset House. The first problem is that you need tickets to even get into the courtyard. I had been hoping to stroll around and hobnob with Vivienne Westwood, etc. Obviously, I don't have a ticket. But that's okay as I can stand just outside.

I spot two trendy-looking girls. They look very "with it", as my grandma would say.

"Hi! Can I pitch my design to you?" I ask.

They are very friendly and agree straight away. They're both fashion photographers so they're in the heart of the fashion world. They might take the Skousers and the Fask to their next shoot and demand Kate Moss wears them on the cover of *Vogue*.

It's time for my pitch. I let them know it's starting, then clear my throat and say, "Cold today, isn't it?"

They agree.

"What's the coldest part of you today?"

"Hands," they both say while rubbing them together.

"No," I say. "Anything else?"

They look a bit stumped. Or it might've been confusion. I find myself touching my own face as a hint.

"Face?" they ask.

"Yes!" I say. They look relieved. "I think it's time we reclaimed the face covering from the baddies. So I present to you the Fask."

I put it on.

One of the girls says, "Bad." I think she meant it in the Michael Jackson good way.

The other girl says, "I've done a shoot with lace face masks." We are totally on the same page creatively.

"It's great for cold face days, bad face days or days you don't want to be recognised if you're a celebrity or out with your mistress or male lover. It's a delightful floral pattern with a contrasting edgy denim trim."

I finish with the slogan. Yes, it has a slogan. "The Fask. Face up to it, it's great."

I wait for maybe some applause or cheering. They look at me, smiling.

"Do you like it?" I ask.

While they don't exactly say yes, I get the impression they do. They even mention Alexander McQueen at one point.

Then they start waving to a friend and saying they have to go. I'll be honest, I don't see anyone waving back at them. But that's okay, as I've still got my Skousers to pitch. It strikes me for the first time that I probably shouldn't be carrying my designs in a M&S carrier bag. It's too late now though.

I spot someone else. Someone else looking "with it". She's also happy to hear my pitch. Time to break out the Skousers.

"Every day we have to make decisions. Toast or cereal, bus or Tube, having children or a terrifyingly lonely old age? I have something to simplify life and reduce the number of decisions. Let me present to you the Skousers. For those days when you can't decide between skirt or trousers."

I pull them out of the M&S carrier bag.

"Also perfect for the days when you can be bothered to shave the front of your legs but can't face doing the back. The Skousers: the best of both worlds."

I give her a broad smile to indicate I've finished.

"Well, they are good for when you can't decide between trousers and skirt," she says.

"Would you be interested in taking any units?"

"I work at a knitwear company," she says.

"You could make woolly ones," I suggest weakly.

She smiles politely and then wishes me luck.

I can't help noticing now that I'm the only person pitching designs outside London Fashion Week. It doesn't seem to be the thing. Still, there's always a first time. And a last time.

I've also noticed that some filming has just started. I'm not sure what channel. There's a yellow foam bit on the mic and something I can't read. It appears to be the kind of TV channel that also doesn't have access into London Fashion Week. These are my kind of people. And they present my one last chance.

I put my Fask on and as soon as the camera is rolling and

the lady reporter is talking I'm right in the background as close as I can get.

Surely, this means my design is going to be on television. Unless they started recording again when I went away. While I've not yet sold my designs, I have created a real buzz around the Skousers and the Fask. They could be the next must-have items. For the hot new creepy, robber-like, colourful Ku Klux Klan, gimp look.

21

The Challenge: To campaign for a four-day working week

Imagine if every week had a bank holiday. If every weekend was three days long. For me, this is way better than imagining there's no heaven or no countries (no offence, John Lennon). And who wouldn't want a four-day working week? Really? Who? Well maybe not Thomas Edison and Margaret Thatcher. But they're both dead. And we've got the light bulb now.

In 1930, the economist John Maynard Keynes predicted that by the twenty-first century we'd be working a fifteen-hour week. The average working week in the UK is now thirty-six hours. Meaning we're all just embarrassing ourselves and failing in the eyes of this eminent man.

I begin this challenge with gusto. I can really make a difference. Make life better.

My first thoughts are of the three-day week in the seventies. Three days is a bit excessive, even for me, but I never understood why it was thought to be such a bad thing. Yes, there was hardly any electricity because of the miners' strike, but candlelight is very flattering. Then I looked into it a bit more and read about how TV had to finish at 10.30 p.m. and I finally understand the true horror.

Although we shouldn't overlook the positive things, like how, during the winter, there was such a severe fuel shortage and it was so cold that women were allowed to turn up to their chilly workplaces wearing trousers instead of skirts. Ahh, the seventies. Different times.

There are other precedents for a shorter working week. In 2013, the President of Gambia brought in a four-day working week to allow Gambians to devote more time to prayers, social activities and agriculture.

I'm not sure about the praying and agriculture bit. I'm also not entirely sure about this president, who used to be a faith healer, once said he was going to rule for a billion years, claims to have invented a herbal cure for HIV that works in three days and insists on his title being His Excellency Sheikh Professor Doctor President, despite having left school at sixteen with five O levels.

I edit him out of my proposal to the UK government. Instead, I focus on how it creates more jobs, means fewer carbon emissions and how a study somewhere, at some time, found that 72% of people would rather work longer days, four days a week. 72%! It's what we all want. And when I say "we", I mean 72% of us. This is great, but maybe one statistic from a study that I can't be bothered to check the credibility of is not enough.

What would be great, what could make all the difference, would be if I could get one of the biggest companies in Britain to say they'll do a four-day week. Then the government would have to take it seriously.

I really study the top-ten biggest companies to see which one would be the most likely to convert to a shorter week. By which I mean I look at all their addresses to see which is closest to my work.

It is BP. The fifth biggest company in the UK with a turnover of £91 billion and employing over 10,000 people in this country. Surely all I need to do is go to their HQ.

Now, I know you can't just show up and ask to speak to the CEO. If I've learned anything at all, it's that you need names.

I do my research. I'm thinking someone in HR is probably my best bet. I find a name on the Internet. I'm just about to go when I remember I'm often asked for business cards in these kinds of circumstances and never have them.

I need a business card showing me to be the CEO of the Four-Day-Week Campaign. I'm wondering if I've got anyone else's card in my purse that I could doctor. I have a look. Nothing. I'm clearly not the type of person who gets given business cards.

But what I do find in my purse is a Caffè Nero loyalty card. I was hoping one side would be blank to write the business stuff on. But they clearly didn't think of this during the design process.

I'm undeterred. I find a receipt (from TGI Fridays) which I can attach to one side of the loyalty card and write on the back of.

There is the slight problem that I don't have any glue or Sellotape, but luckily I have a hairgrip in my bag so I slide that on.

I design a nice logo for the corner. I'd describe it as a mess of the characters 4, D and W. I cast a critical eye over the mess and then add a smiley face in the corner. All I need to do now is write "Annabel Port, CEO, Four-Day-Week Campaign", my email address and mobile number, and I'm ready to go.

I arrive at reception and tell the lady confidently who I'm here to see.

"You're here to see Adriano?" Her tone leaves no doubt that this is definitely a question, not a confirming statement.

I'm wondering what's weird about me seeing him. Me in my jeans and parka and messy hair at one of the biggest oil companies in the world.

I assure her I am. She takes my name and calls up. I wait to be asked all the usual questions, like: do you have an appointment? But they don't come. She hangs up and says he's coming down. She tells me to take a seat and gives me a visitor pass.

This is very unusual. I don't even have to wait long. He arrives in just a few minutes. He's very smart-looking and seems confused when he sees me. I start wishing I'd brushed my hair.

But he's walking right towards me and it might look strange, me dragging a comb though my hair while shaking hands.

Instead, while his hand clasps mine, I say brightly, "Hi. I'm Annabel Port, the CEO of the Four-Day-Week Campaign. I'll be liaising with the government regarding the changeover to a four-day working week."

The government thing is not a lie. I do intend on talking to them tomorrow.

He looks really confused now.

"Sorry, who have you been talking to here about this?" he asks.

"You," I say.

"Me?"

"Yes," I say. Then pause. "Now."

I get out my business card as I'm worried I'm losing him. He takes it. And lifts up the receipt to clearly show the Caffè Nero card.

"Oh, don't look there," I say quickly.

Then I try and distract him with more talk about the four-day week. I'm really babbling now and I'm very aware of that as I hear myself use the word "directive" and I don't even really know what that means.

"Look," he tells me, "we do have agile working here. But let me get you a business card and then you can email me with all this. I've got yours so I'll keep this."

He puts my card in his pocket and walks off to get his.

I'm panicking now. That Caffè Nero loyalty card is nearly full. I want it back. I'm two stamps away from a free coffee.

He's gone ages. When he does come back, he hands me his card and tells me to email.

"Have you still got my card?" I ask.

"Yes," he says patting his pocket.

"Can I have the underneath back?"

He's unable to control an outburst of laughter. It's an awkward moment but he does return it to me.

My only problem is that he keeps the hairgrip I used to attach the receipt to the card. Those are really cheap, though, so I take the hit, figuring I can claim it back from expenses when my four-day-week company really takes off.

And now that I've got really strong interest from one of the UK's biggest employers, I'm ready to tackle the government tomorrow.

I start the day full of optimism. I just need to present my overwhelming evidence to the government, which I'm imagining will have a quick look and then we'll be all sorted for the week after next.

I'm guessing I need to approach Iain Duncan Smith as he's the head of the Department for Work and Pensions. And the good news is he was heckled during a speech and called a ratbag in Edinburgh the day before, so is probably feeling a bit fragile, a bit needy, a bit eager to please right now. The timing couldn't be more perfect.

I find the number and call up. The phone rings for ever. I'm holding on for about five minutes. And I suspect by the tone of voice of the woman who eventually answers that she had been just sitting there, waiting for me to give up.

I ask to speak to Iain Duncan Smith.

"What sort of enquiry is it?" she asks.

I explain I'm from the Four-Day-Week Campaign.

"And you are?"

"I'm Annabel, the CEO."

"CEO of what?"

"The Four-Day-Week Campaign," I say patiently.

I'm worried her mind is not fully on the job.

She tells me she'll see if his office will take my call. I'm on hold now. The hold music is medieval but played on a very cheap synthesizer. It's quite some noise.

Eventually the receptionist comes back and says everyone is in a meeting today. An all-day meeting. Involving everyone. I'm suspicious, but relax a little when she gives me the email address for Iain Duncan Smith.

He's got quite a weird email address as it starts with "ministers@". But maybe IDS was already taken.

I send him this:

Dear Iain Duncan Smith,

Firstly, I don't think you're a rat bag. In fact, I think you are a hamster bag. Looking all sweet, while endlessly running on a wheel, getting nowhere because of all the restrictions you face – money, staff shortages, maybe the idiocy of your superiors. You're there, biting away at the bars of your cage, hoping for the freedom to fulfil all your desires, fat-cheeked and passionate.

I've gone on about the hamster thing for longer than I meant to there. So, straight to the point. I'm the CEO of the Four-Day-Week Campaign. It's working in Gambia at the moment. Perhaps you'd consider emulating the President of Gambia (but perhaps not in making out you've invented a herbal HIV cure or insisting everyone call you His Excellency Sheikh Professor Doctor President).

But anyway, it's going well there. Probably. I'll admit I've not checked it out. But it's not in the news so let's assume it's going well.

Therefore, our campaign proposes we also have a four-day week. BP (the company, not Billie Piper) have said they are interested in this and they are one of the biggest companies in the UK. I've been in long talks with HR there and they are pretty excited about this proposal.

Now, you're probably worrying about what we're all going to do with our extra day off. Thinking we'll be lying about on urine-soaked mattresses and doing nothing but boosting the smack trade. Well then, you have a very low opinion of the British public. Our plan for the first few

months of the new regime is to challenge Croatia for
the title of World's Longest Sausage, by making our own
longer version to enter into the *Guinness Book of Records*.

Well please do get back in touch today by 7 p.m. at the
very, very latest as I've got to report back to the board.

Many thanks and all best wishes,

Annabel Port

CEO, Four-Day-Week Campaign

P.S. Oh and it will create jobs.

Annoyingly, he's not got back to me, but he's probably busy
calling round the companies of Britain telling them about the
new regime. So get ready to make the world's largest sausage.
Or lie about on a urine-soaked mattress all day. Your choice.

22

The Challenge: To have my portrait painted by a major artist

This won't be my first portrait. My first one was twenty-two years ago. Unfortunately, I can't use this as it was a nude that my boyfriend at the time did for GCSE art, which caused a bit of a stir when it was displayed in the corridor of his all-boys' school. And my then boyfriend didn't go on to become a major artist. Or even an artist.

But the good news is I have experience of having my portrait done. Experience of sitting still, that is. I just need to find a major artist.

I make a list of all the ones I know that are alive.

- Tracy Emin
- Banksy
- Damien Hirst
- Neil Buchanan
- That old lady who messed up the fresco of Jesus's face when trying to restore it in Spain.

That's it. I'm not in any way an expert on art. I know nothing and I'm not sure any of these people would want to do my portrait.

I try to find some other artists and my research reveals that there are portrait painters out there, but they're not that famous. I can sort of see why. Why would you do a portrait when you have really great photography now?

I'm quite keen on the man who did the recent Kate Middleton portrait, because everyone hated it apart from Kate, who said it was amazing. Even though it did look like she'd just done a twenty-year stretch in prison.

I quite like the idea I'd get to be this well-mannered and magnanimous as I rarely am either of these things in everyday life.

I find out his name is Paul Emsley and that he spent three and a half months on Kate's portrait. I've got three days to have the portrait done and hung in a major place. This is a bit worrying.

I move on to a woman called Isobel Peachey, who did a portrait of the Queen three years ago that was hung on a cruise liner, which is a bit of a weird place for a portrait. They must be constantly straightening it. But it is a really good portrait. I really like it, it's nice and bright and the Queen looks good, not at all manly.

I manage to have some email contact with her but she's busy this week, even though I say she could just do a quick pencil drawing and I'll colour it in for her. I even get as far as sending her a holiday picture of me to work from. Communication ends after that. I wish I'd been able to find a holiday photo where I wasn't nude. Not really! I was fully dressed by a lake. But it did end the conversation.

I manage to find another portrait painter though, someone called Nicky Philipps. I think she did the one of the Queen looking like a bloke in the wig. That's the critics' words, not mine.

When I google her I find that she's represented by an agency, so I call them up.

"Hi, I'm calling about Nicky Philipps. I'd like her to do my portrait."

"Yes, of course," the woman says.

This is easy! But then she goes on to say she's quite booked up at the moment and the earliest would be in seven months. My deadline is Thursday.

But just in case she can squeeze me in this afternoon I ask how much it'll be.

It's £19,000 plus VAT.

"Is that coloured in?" I ask.

There's a pause then she says, "Yes, that's oil, so yes, it's in colour."

I tell her I was hoping to have it done for tomorrow so I might call back.

I'm a bit worried now. Then I realise something. Geoff said I had to have my portrait done by a major artist. But he didn't say when they had to be a major artist. What if I have my portrait done by someone who is a major artist in the future?

And I know where to find a future major artist. Art school. I head off to the art school that's the closest to work.

It doesn't look quite how I imagined. I thought there'd be stone pillars at the very least, but actually it looks more like an English language school.

I try not to let the lack of grandeur put me off. I go in. There's a corridor before the reception. It's all very empty.

Then I see a girl coming towards me. She looks like an art student as she's holding some rolled-up thick paper.

"Hi. Are you a student here?" I ask. She is.

"Will you do my portrait for me?"

I hold my A5 lined notebook and biro out to her, while wishing I'd thought to turn up with some proper paper and a nice pencil or some charcoal or something.

But the girl says, "Oh, okay."

This girl is amazing. The type of person who is willing to do the portrait of a complete stranger, there and then, is the type of person who will become a major artist.

I offer to hold the rolled-up thick paper for her but she tucks it under her arm. She's willing to draw me but not trust me.

Her eyes are flicking up at me then down to the paper, and she's drawing away. I'm smiling, as I want to look nice in my portrait and my resting face is very melancholic.

Time passes very slowly when a stranger is drawing you in a corridor. I felt like I was there for about fifteen minutes but it was probably only about three.

And then she's finished. She signs it with "Misa". She seems embarrassed by it but hands it over. It's good. Apart from I'm not mad on the eyebrows. I had them threaded at the weekend but she makes them look very untidy.

But, remembering Kate Middleton's good manners, I tell her I love it and she's got a bright future, she's going to do great. This might just be the confidence boost she needs to become a major artist.

She took a photo of it, which was nice. And then it was a bit awkward as she was leaving and so was I. I had to really power-walk off so we didn't have to walk together.

Now I just need to get it hung in a major gallery and it obviously has to be the National Portrait Gallery. With portraits of William Shakespeare, Queen Elizabeth I and, soon, me, done in biro on a ripped out bit of an A5 notebook.

I decide to really help them out by framing it, as I've got a spare IKEA one at home. I frame it on the Tube. I feel like it gets admiring looks. They could also be interpreted as "looks".

I'm on my way to the gallery when I realise that I can pretend to be an arty type, a bit airy-fairy, which might mean that I can get away with more.

I arrive at the reception. There's a man behind the desk. I say to him, "Hi. I've got the Misa portrait that's going to be hung today."

"Oh," he says. "Well, who are you here to see? Have you got a name?"

Now is my chance to be a bit arty.

"No, I don't use names."

The man repeats back, "You don't use names."

"No, I don't work with names. Not something I do. Sorry," I say with my warmest smile.

"Okay," he says slowly, "that does make things a little difficult. Three hundred people work here."

I try and distract him from the name issue by getting the portrait out to show him. There's no visible reaction. Instead he tells me he'll make a call and can he take my name.

"Annabel Port," I say without thinking. He repeats it back to me, but to his credit, he doesn't pick me up on the fact I'm happy to use my own name.

He makes some calls but is clearly not getting anywhere. He asks me, "Is the portrait for a collection? Or a competition?"

"No. It's a Misa," I say, like someone might say, "It's a Picasso."

He politely asks no further questions and instead makes another call. He tells a lady my full name and the situation but not that I won't use names, just that I don't have a name. Then passes the phone to me.

The lady is asking questions about my contact and how I was corresponding with them. I tell her it was by phone and she says she'll come down to talk to me.

I sit and wait. I wait a really long time. Long enough, I slowly realise, for this woman to google my name. This could be humiliating. What am I doing? I'm wasting the time of people with proper jobs.

I realise I can't cope with being confronted. I tell the man on the front desk that I need to make a call and I go.

But I don't go very far. I'm not giving up. Do I really need this woman's permission to display my portrait in the National Portrait Gallery? Probably, is the answer, but I ignore that.

I go into the gallery. I wander round and find a room with an exhibition by Jonathan Yeo. There are lots of celebrity por-traits grouped together. I don't recognise them all so maybe some of them are normal people.

The bottom row is hung quite low to the ground, which is perfect. I get my portrait out and l lean it on the ground against the wall.

An older lady in a lilac raincoat and a beret-like hat takes a closer look. She must know about art if she wears a beret.

It seems to be going down quite well. Nobody is throwing rotten tomatoes at it. A few people stop to take a proper look.

Then a member of staff comes up to me and, pointing at the portrait, says, "Is this yours?"

I consider denying it. But it is a portrait of me. And I'm proud of it. I say, "Yes."

"Could you keep it with you as I've had security calling me," she says.

"Oh right, yes, fine," I say.

They just want me to keep it with me, but that doesn't mean I can't stand holding it up by the other portraits on the wall. Surprisingly, this seems to be fine. I have no further complaints. My arms hurt a bit after a while, but the room gets quite busy and I display my portrait to a lot of people.

It would seem I really did have my portrait done by a (future) major artist and displayed in a major gallery.

Q&A 2

More questions you might be
asking yourself

I quite enjoyed talking to myself before, once I'd edited out "you're worthless", "why are you doing this, nobody is going to read it" and "you're wasting your life". Here's more of the Q&A.

Is your flat really that bad?

If you came round, you'd probably think that it's not that bad. But that's because I'd have spent the week cleaning and tidying in anticipation of your visit. When I moved in it was in a nice condition, but not decorated to my taste. I was telling a friend about how I'd have to redecorate and she said, "Why don't you just change your taste? It'd be a lot easier." So I did. And she was right, it was a lot easier.

It turns out if you just leave the garden, though, it changes quite a lot. I do worry that I'm that woman with the jungle front garden that all the kids on the street are scared of and tell each other that I'm a witch.

The thing I probably should've changed is the pre-pay electricity meter. You don't usually find one in the house of someone with a job and mortgage. I think it's a nice glimpse into what my life will be like when I get found out to be a talentless fraud who should never have got a job in radio. It's also seems to quite annoy Geoff, so that's the main reason I've not changed it.

What's Geoff like?

When he's not showing disdain for my pre-paid electricity, frugality, wearing Topshop clothes that "are not age-appropriate", the fact that I don't eat meat but I do eat fish, and refusing to believe that I had the primary school nickname of The Flying Flea, claiming instead that it was actually Hamble after the creepy doll from *Playschool*, he is lovely.

He's big-hearted, enormously clever and extremely generous, and I'd probably be living in a gutter if not for him. Just never play Monopoly with him. He's a commie bastard who won't buy property and hands his money out at random intervals. It's infuriating.

Do you think maybe you should get a real job?

I'd probably have to go on an adult-education computer course first.

But yes, there are moments, like when I'm pretending to be Councillor Drugget from *The Brittas Empire* on a Wednesday afternoon, that I wonder if my time could not be better spent.

Yes, about that – do you worry that you are wasting other people's time? People with real jobs, making a real contribution to society?

The best I can hope for is that it gives the people involved something to talk about when they get home from work. "So today someone came into the leisure centre and they were pretending to be someone called Councillor Drugget and kept calling me Gordon and they said *Songs of Praise* was being filmed there. It was kind of annoying as it interrupted me from finalising the figures for a big charity event at the centre that would've raised millions and I won't have time to go back to it now, so it's being cancelled. It was really weird. Why would someone do that?"

Yes, I worry about it all the time.

Have you ever said no to one of Geoff's challenges?

Once. He challenged me to join the Harlem Globetrotters. I'm five foot three! I live in London! I was quite good at netball when I was eleven, though. When I definitely, definitely had the nickname of The Flying Flea. Perhaps I should've done it.

And travel to Harlem? I can't help noticing you don't like to travel too far from your work or home for these challenges. Why is that?

Lack of time, laziness. All the usual reasons.

Some of the things you do are really embarrassing. Don't you get embarrassed?

When I'm doing the more brazen, ridiculous things, I become someone else in my head. A more naive, innocent version of myself. I'm also so good at lying to myself that I often start to become convinced I really am, for example, starting work that day as the assistant Ravenmaster and can start to feel quite indignant that nobody seems to know about it. Lying to yourself is a good skill to have. I'm pretty sure it's the only way anyone has the confidence to do anything.

We're about three-quarters of the way through the book now. What would you say you'd learned now?
Again? Really? Okay.

1. If you're not in contact with someone from the past any more, it's because they don't want to see you anymore. Contacting them is embarrassing for you and for them. Don't do it. Just leave it.
2. If you're going to turn up at a big company, or any company, wanting to talk to someone about something, it's best to do some research first and come armed with a name of someone who works there. It took me a worryingly long time to work this out. It also helps to have a business card, even if you've made it yourself out of a Caffè Nero card and a TGI Fridays receipt.
3. Warwick University really will make no exceptions for anyone. They are very rigid. I feel a lot better about them rejecting me all those years ago.
4. People at work are always in meetings. Either that, or a good way to avoid speaking to someone is to pretend you are in a meeting.
5. I really have no shame.

23

The Challenge:
To expose some Internet fraud

I'm no stranger to an online investigation. I've been known to carry out some heavy-duty googling and facebooking to work out if various boyfriends have been cheating on me. The things I've found out! How hard can this be? Especially as I've always thought that the people writing these email scams can't be too bright. They all seem so obviously fake.

However, the first thing I learn is that they are written really badly on purpose, to draw out only the most very gullible who might give out their bank details. And there are lot of very gullible people; these email scams made $9.3 billion in 2009.

I've realised what I've got to do. If I appear very gullible and not so bright, I could trick an email scam fraudster. Trick them into giving me their details and then I can fly to Nigeria or wherever and confront them. If I can get enough money for the flight from petty cash at work.

I just need to find an email scam now. It's not hard. I just go straight to my spam folder, where one catches my eye. It's from a David Ellis, who claims to be the Head of Inspection Unit at the United Nations Inspection Agency. That's a lot of inspection going on there. But what's he inspecting?

I soon find out. It's an abandoned shipment. "$4 million or more" in two metal trunk boxes weighing approximately 110kg each that had been transferred from John F. Kennedy Airport to their facility in Atlanta. I'm slightly unclear why, but presumably for inspection.

The email goes on to reveal that it was abandoned by a diplomat from the United Kingdom who hadn't wanted to pay the non-inspection fees. Those inspection fees must be astronomical to justify abandoning $4 million or more.

Weirder still, it emerges that my name and email address were on the documents. If I can reconfirm my details and then either pick up the abandoned shipment or arrange for its delivery, I can have it.

There is a catch though. *I am ready to assist you in any way I can for you to get back this packages provided you will also give me something out of it (financial gratification).*

I'm glad of the information in the brackets. I hadn't been quite sure what he meant.

I set about writing a reply. First I set up an email account under the name Millicent Frender and with the address of cleverestclogs@gmail.com. Nobody actually clever would have that as their email address. And cleverclogs@gmail.com was already taken.

Then I get ready to write something that is going to lure him into my web. While his name is David Ellis, it appears he shortens it to Dellis.

Dear Dellis,

I need that thing you emailed about. I'm very keen to
pick it up. Or arrange for someone to carry it to me.

I've moved into a house with no built-in cupboards, so
the two metal trunk boxes would be perfect for extra
storage space.

Please could you send me a picture (photo or
drawing) so that I can see if they'll look nice stacked up in
my living room. The alternative is to put them under my
bed.

As I'll be putting things like a spare duvet, winter
jumpers, a badminton racquet, some old vinyl, an
unwanted gift and the guest Teasmade in it, could you
please ensure they come to me empty, i.e., take the
money out.

Hope to hear from you today. As otherwise I'll see
what Argos have.

Lots of love,
   Millicent Frender (Mrs)

I hear back in two hours. His response makes me wonder
if he'd actually read my email. He writes:

Dear –

And then nothing. Not my name. Followed by,

I got your email and Noted concerning the shipment
of your consignment of Trunk Boxes which will take
effect within the next 72 hours once the confirmation of
relevant documents and clearance of the trunk boxes.

He goes on more about the money, about the denominations and how it's stacked up. I think Dellis is getting a bit carried away with himself. Then he says other stuff that doesn't make much sense before asking for $570. But this is the delivery costs, not the financial gratification. I do find myself worrying about his gratification.

I reply with this:

Hi Dellis,

Thank you for your email. But can you confirm that the two metal trunks will be delivered EMPTY? Without the money. I need them to be empty so I can put all my things in. I'm hoping one will be long enough for my ironing board as this is currently just leaning against the wall in the kitchen and looks untidy.

Please let me know.

Many thanks,

Millicent Frender (Mrs)

There's no reply. I'm worried he's become suspicious. I really want to confront him, Roger Cook-style, so I do some heavy-duty detective work.

All I've got is an email address. A Yahoo one that ends in ".ph", which indicates it's from the Philippines. Even though he'd said he was in Atlanta, Georgia. But maybe he's on holiday and isn't very good at switching off from work.

There's more I can discover though, by tracking his IP address. This isn't easy for me, but eventually I have the exact location where the email was sent from.

It's not Atlanta. It's not the Philippines. It's Lagos in Nigeria: 51% of scam emails come from Nigeria and this one is no exception.

The net is closing in on David Ellis. I know where he is; I

just need to confront him. For this, I really need a telephone number. But because I think he's now suspicious about Millicent Frender, I decide to set up another email address.

My new one is littleoldlady1901@gmail.com and her name is Frail Weakminded. I put in the profile a picture of a frail old lady. As I'm setting up the account I get so into character that I struggle a bit with the verification code. Once it's ready, I send David Ellis an email.

Dear Dellis,

I cannot thank your kindness enough. That shipment of money will be life-changing. I live in terrible poverty with no friends or family.

I worry a bit now that if I'm in terrible poverty, I wouldn't have a computer or the Internet, so I add:

I'm at the local library using the Internet.

Please send me your telephone number to discuss shipment.

God bless you.

Frail

While I'm waiting for reply, so that I'm not putting all my eggs in one basket, I decide to try and investigate another email in my spam folder. I see one from a Gareth and Catherine Bull. Their names ring a bell so I read on.

My wife and I won the Euro Millions Lottery of 41 Million British Pounds and we have decided to donate 1.5 million British Pounds to 6 individuals worldwide as our own charity project.

That's who they are! The EuroMillions winners. The email helpfully gives a link to an interview with Gareth and Catherine Bull that was in the *Daily Mail* after they won the jackpot. I'm sure that is exactly what the Bulls would do if it was really them writing this email. It goes on,

> Your email address was among the emails which were
> submitted to us by the Google, Inc as a web user, which
> was used for the draw with an electronic balloting system
> your email address came out as the 4th lucky beneficiary
> world wide.

Who knew that Google have this email address randomiser machine? They then ask me to send my full name, mobile number, age and country. Not my bank details yet though.

First of all, I trace the email to New Delhi, India. Then I decide to write a reply that cleverly draws them out and exposes them. That is the plan. What actually happens is I get really carried away.

> Gaz and Cathy – I cannot believe how weird this
> coincidence is. It's Annabel from the Costa Brava, 1991!
> We met on holiday and had the best time together.
>
> And now by some random twist of fate my name gets
> pulled out of the Google randomiser to get some of your
> money.
>
> What a thrill. Do you remember my husband Shane?
> What a night we had on the last night. Wink wink!!
> Unfortunately it seems that one of you gave Shane
> herpes, but don't worry, we had a good laugh about it.

What was slightly less funny is I that contracted a baby that night. Yes! Who knows if it's Shane's or yours, Gaz?!? We could do a DNA test if you want. I've been meaning to get in touch and let you know but life gets in the way, doesn't it?

Anyway, I most certainly wouldn't dream of taking any of your money. Keep it to yourself – have fun. Just let me know about the DNA test thing. And if you want any photos of the child (now aged 22).

Well, can't wait to hear back – can you believe this has happened?!!!

Annabel xxxx

I'm sitting wondering if this was the kind of thing that Roger Cook did in his hard-hitting investigations when I notice that Frail Weakminded has a new email. It's a reply from David Ellis. With his telephone number.

I dial it straight away but it's not working. It seems to be missing an international dialling code. I google the first three digits and it does appear to be an Atlanta number. I try it with a USA code and it works. I respect Dellis for this. This is clever, he's somehow redirected it.

The bad news, though, is it goes to answerphone. I leave a message. I put on an elderly, quavery voice and say, "Hello? David? It's Frail. I just wanted to speak about the payment. Maybe you could call me."

I give my work phone number and wait. Nothing. Frail sends him another email saying the number goes to answerphone and leaving the number again for him to call.

Forty-five minutes later he replies. He says he needs the

$570 for the "delivery of my consignment to commence".

I need to speak to him for the confrontation though. I email back:

I can call you now? Or you call me? Then I make payment.

I wait. Nothing. No response. I write again:

How do I make payment? I'm scared of losing the money.

Nothing. I'm starting to feel like I'm the spammer and he's the victim.

I don't hear from him again for another hour. It's after five o'clock when I do.

He says:

Dear Frail, Thanks for your email, i try call but not going through, this is my direct cell : +404 826 0722 dial the number in this way and call me immediately.

Then he gives me the details of where to wire the $570.

I can't call him at this time as we're doing the radio show. I can probably try when the news is on. I write:

I'm just stirring gruel so will call in 15 minutes.

He replies, being quite insistent on the whole wiring thing. It's like he's not that fussed about the phone call.

He's using the expressions, "Guarantee you that you will not loose your fund," and, "This is real and legit."

I still can't call back yet, so I stall him with:

Okay I'm just getting my life savings out from under the mattress.

He replies with:

I assured you that once you send the clearance and delivery fee your consignment will deliver to your doorstep without any problem or more cost okay, I promised you with name of God.

A weird thing is happening now. I'm sort of starting to believe him. He is very convincing. Then I remember the UN Inspection agency and the diplomat who didn't want to pay the non-inspection fee and how two metal trunks with "$4million or more" inside have been abandoned with only my name and email address on the paperwork. I'm ready to call him.

I dial the number. He answers!

"Hello, David? It's Frail," I say in my quavery voice.

"Hello Frail."

We spend a lot of time now saying, "How are you?" He really does seem to care how I am.

Then he starts going on about the consignment again. I deal the first killer blow.

"I'm a bit confused, my grandson said your IP address means you are in Nigeria."

"Okay, Madame Frail," he replies. "So you need to wire the $570."

"Is this a trick?" I say. My voice is gradually going from little old lady to interrogatory and Roger Cook-like.

"No, no," he assures me. "Your name was on the consignment paperwork."

"But you sent the email to lots of people."

"No, no. You have my office email address, the AOL one."

I'm no expert but I suspect the United Nations doesn't use AOL.

I get ready to deal the final killer blow. It's the moment I've been building up to. I need to be fearless here. I completely break cover and confront Dellis. I say, "I think you should stop doing this and do something else."

Then I hang up.

I think that at this moment, investigative journalism just hit rock bottom.

But maybe Dellis heard those words and thought, *Perhaps I should stop doing this and do something else.* Maybe he did. And there's no denying that I exposed an Internet fraudster. Or at the very least, just wasted a little bit of his time.

24

The Challenge: To bring the spirit of Brazil to the UK

Brazilians seem to be relaxed, happy people who love others and love life. They are spontaneous, free, liberated and unrepressed. They are the exact opposite of me. It's going to be a big challenge for me to bring the Brazilian spirit to the UK.

I'm struggling to even check if I'm right, as when I google "Brazilian spirit" it just returns endless pages about cachaça, the spirit that's in caipirinhas, their national cocktail.

I do learn about how chilled out the Brazilians are, though. For one, they have a national cocktail. I also discover online that when they're waiting for a bus, they're thinking, *The bus might come, the bus might not come.*

If I'm waiting for a Tube and it's more than five minutes away, I'm filled with rage. I don't think I'm alone.

But I get the opportunity to try out this new mindset very soon. I'm walking to my train station and I'm pretty much there when I see my train coming. I'd normally run to make it. Today, I just keep strolling. Even when I see there's not another train for six minutes. I'm going through the barriers when it's leaving. There's a man behind me. A good few metres behind me so I slow down a bit, then say, "Who cares that we missed that train?"

He makes a "mmm" noise with a smile.

"It's only six minutes to the next one. If it comes," I say.

He makes the same noise. It's like he fears that actual words would encourage me.

"*Que sera sera*," I say.

He doesn't even do the "mmm" this time. He just gives me a weak smile.

There's no denying though that on a very small scale, I've brought the spirit of Brazil to my train station.

Once I'm in town, I decide to continue with this new chilled-out me and start spreading my vibe. I'm so chilled out I'm using the words "chilled out" and "vibe", when normally if these kinds of words entered my mind I'd bristle with irritation. I can definitely help others and I know where. A traffic jam. People get really angry in those. I've seen the film *Falling Down* so I know this.

I go to Regent Street and immediately see a line of cars. Admittedly it's more of a stopping at a red-light situation than an actual traffic jam, but people get road rage in all sorts of different situations these days. I can help. I can bring the vibe of Copacabana beach to a congested road in central London.

I'm briefly concerned that nobody has their windows wound down, but it doesn't stop me.

I knock on a window of a car with an attractive woman in

it. She turns to look but makes no moves to wind down the window. That's okay. As I can shout.

"BE CHILLED, YEAH. NO RUSH!"

I feel bad about two things. Firstly, saying "no rush" when maybe there is a rush. Maybe she's rushing to an ailing relative's hospital bedside. Or to give birth. Secondly, I feel bad about saying, "be chilled, yeah", as I sound like an idiot. Perhaps wisely, she ignores me. There a black cab behind her.

"*QUE SERA SERA!*" I shout at that driver. He gives me a thumbs up, which is nice. I imagine there's lots of thumbs up in Brazil. I'm beginning to wonder why anyone would go to Brazil when you can completely recreate the spirit here.

Unfortunately, the traffic jam is easing off now as the light has turned green. But it's probably not enough for everyone to just be chilled out. There's probably a bit more to Brazil than that. I need to learn more about their spirit.

I investigate these Brazilians further and I learn a lot. I learn they brush their teeth not just morning and night but after lunch. Maybe their lack of inhibition is down to their fresh breath.

I learn they've got a word, "*saudade*", that has no English equivalent. It means a strong desire for something that does not exist or is unattainable. How can there not be an English word for this? I live in constant state of *saudade*. *Saudade* for happiness and untold wealth and less-bandy legs.

I discover that on escalators in Brazil there are no rules, they don't wear black to funerals and they eat an avocado like a fruit.

I also learn that when a Brazilian meets someone for the first time, they will always invite them to their home for drinks or dinner. But as it's common understanding that this never actually happens, the invite is never taken up. This is amazing. All the politeness but none of the suffering of having to cook for someone and clean your toilet before they arrive.

I can definitely try out some of these things. The escalator one will be easy. Yet when it comes to it, on the Tube escalators, I can't do it. I can walk up the standing side but I can't stand on the walking side. It's impossible for me. I can't be that despised person. In all the things I've done, I've found my limit. I can't be chaotically Brazilian on an escalator.

It's okay, I console myself, there are lots of other things on the list. I love the inviting strangers you've just met to your home but knowing they'll never come. The only problem is I don't tend to meet new people in my everyday life. Then I remember somewhere where everyone is really overfriendly. The clothes shop French Connection. They seem to have a policy that every single member of staff has to greet you and ask if they can help you. If you're ever lonely, go there.

Today is no different at French Connection. Straight away a lady says hello and asks if I want any help. And because I'm in the Brazilian state of mind, even though I really don't want any help, I have to say yes. These free-spirited Brazilians say yes to everything.

There's a pause where she waits for me to say what I want help with. When that doesn't come, she asks how she can help.

It's a bit awkward but I have to admit, "I didn't mean it, sorry."

To cover the awkwardness, I launch straight into, "But it's been lovely meeting you. If you ever want to come to my house for dinner or drinks, it'd be great to have you."

She laughs very, very nervously. When the laugh stops there's just fear in her eyes. I smile, wander off, look at one item of clothing, then leave. I look at the one thing to appear normal, like I wasn't just going in there to invite her round my house. I'm not sure it worked.

There's one more thing left to try. I've not yet brought to the UK the crazy Brazilian party spirit. Every day is carnival day in Brazil, I think. I need to bring these wild, chaotic, party times here.

This is a bit more me. I like a party. But only after at least two glasses of wine. Mainly because while sober I can't dance, look anyone in the eye or kiss anyone on the lips. I'm aware there are three words for this: repressed and drink problem.

It's a worry how I'm going to do this sober. On a Thursday lunchtime. But I've got to get the Brazilian spirit here, and preferably somewhere really boring and sombre, so even the slightest hint of party spirit will seem like Rio Carnival in comparison. I'm not keen on a library or graveyard, though. I just need a very peaceful area of London and it strikes me that Gray's Inn Gardens could be perfect. It's in Chancery Lane, where lots of sombre lawyers work, probably spending all day reading thick, dusty, leather-bound books. But they've got to take a break at some point and I'm sure this green space is where they go.

When I arrive, it's not quite what I imagined. It's not all lawyers taking a break from dusty books. One man is wearing a football shirt.

There is also a really posh bit, a fancy cafe in an open-sided marquee. I consider going in there but it looks like it's lawyers meeting with clients and what if I jeopardised something big like Jarndyce vs Jarndyce or Kramer vs Kramer?

I look around at the people sitting on the grass. I see three sitting down drinking Pimm's. They're clearly the work-hard, play-hard types. Maybe they've just won a big landmark case. This makes it easier; they're already a bit lubricated but not yet wild.

There's a lady in a nice wraparound dress and two men in pastel-coloured shirts. One pink, one mauve. Neither are wearing ties. I walk towards them with a smile. Mauve shirt man spots me and smiles back.

I've not prepared what I'm going to say as it's too painful to plan ahead. I decide to be spontaneous and this is what comes out of my mouth when I'm by their group: "Party time! Let's go! Uh uh uh uh uh!" Every "uh" was punctuated by me punching a fist forward. I've never made this noise or done this move before. I have no idea where it came from. It could've been the most excruciating moment ever. But they laugh and go, "Yeah!" They are not horrified. They might even be kind of enjoying our interaction.

I keep going. "Let's samba!" I then remember I don't know how to samba, so add, "Can you samba?"

"I can," says wraparound dress lady.

"Teach me how! I can't do it," I say.

I can tell she immediately regrets saying she knew how.

She says, "I've had a couple of drinks, I've probably forgotten now."

I immediately have fears for her career – with a memory this delicate combined with a lunchtime Pimm's habit – but I gracefully say nothing.

Now pink-shirt man is saying, "It's all in the hips."

"Yeah," I agree, moving my hips from side to side. "Come on, let's do it!" I'm really trying to keep the energy up.

"Maybe after a few more drinks," they tell me.

"Okay, I'm coming back!" I say, trying to sound non-threatening.

I walk away to decide what to do next, how to keep this crazy Brazilian party in the park going. I sit for a few minutes, during which I notice them leave. But it is 2 p.m.; they probably had to go back to work. I'm sure that's it.

A lot of the area is emptying now, so I call it a day as I'm exhausted from being Brazilian. If I lived there, I'd have to take naps every two hours. I leave and go to the Tube station. The train is due in four minutes. I silently fume.

25

The Challenge: To collect more tax from the super-rich

There's not a person alive who'd be shocked to discover that the super-rich have been avoiding tax. Apart from the Chancellor George Osborne, who has expressed some surprise that this has been going on. He just couldn't believe they aren't paying the same amount of tax as the rest of us. That, on average, they are only paying 10% tax. He was flabbergasted. Something needs to be done. And while George Osborne is in a state of shock, Geoff believes I can help. In these times of economic woe, I can chase the super-rich for more tax. A bit like Robin Hood, but stealing from the rich to give to HMRC. And maybe not actually stealing.

I know who I want to target. Sir Philip Green. His name is always coming up in relation to tax. He's Mr High Street Shop man, the chairman of the Arcadia Group, which owns Topshop and BHS, among others. He's always hanging around with Kate Moss and he definitely qualifies as super-rich. His son had a £4 million bar mitzvah.

I head straight to the headquarters of his company Arcadia. I've not got a clear plan in my head on how I plan to collect the money, but I figure once I'm face-to-face with him, something will come to mind.

It's getting to the face-to-face bit that might be tricky. But I have an idea. If I go to reception and say Kate Moss is here to see him, he'll come straight down. My only concern is that there's a high chance that she'll actually be up there with him.

Obviously, there is the problem that I don't look anything at all like Kate Moss, but I find if you say anything with enough confidence, you can often get away with it.

I say to the young man at the reception, "I'm here to see Philip Green."

"And your name is?"

I give him a look intending to convey, *We both know what my name is,* then say, "Kate Moss."

No reaction. At all. He's on the phone now. I can hear him saying, "I've got Kate Moss here to see Sir Philip."

He does a bit of nodding, then passes the phone over to me.

A woman says, "Hi Kate!" She's very friendly. I think she thinks I am Kate Moss. I try and remember what Kate sounds like. It's not easy as I don't think I've ever heard her speak. I know she's from Croydon though so I try and get something of that in my voice.

"Hi!" I say.

"Kate, I'm so sorry, but he's not here. He's overseas."

"Nooo! Where?"

"In the States."

"Nightmare!" I say loudly, and perhaps more coarsely than Kate would.

"Do you want me to say you popped by?" she asks.

I think about it for a moment, then say, "Yes," and hand the phone back.

This has not gone well. I may have got away with impersonating Kate Moss but I've not collected any tax. On the spur of the moment I say to the receptionist, "Have you got a present for me?"

He looks confused. Understandably so. I try and help him out with, "Anything at all that you want to give me?" I'm not sure how helpful that was. He's looking about in a slight panic.

"Any stationery?" I suggest.

"I've got a highlighter pen," he says.

"Great, thanks!"

A highlighter pen is a start but I could probably do with collecting some more tax. Sir Philip's Topshop is very close by. It's obviously a risk going in there since I was banned. What if they call the police? I just have to hope that the security guards have not been studying my photo recently.

I go in and straight to the tills. "Could I have a couple of hangers?" I ask.

The guy shrugs, then gets me two. I shove them in my bag.

BHS is a few doors down. This is also part of Arcadia. I go to the till there.

"Hi, I've been sent from head office to pick up a spare till roll."

She gets me one. I walk out with it.

Sir Philip Green may not be paying as much tax as we'd all like him to, but as of today he is down a highlighter pen, two hangers and a BHS till roll, which I now just need to take to the Treasury.

At the reception there I say to the man, "Annabel Port here to see George Osborne."

"The Chancellor?" he asks.

I suspect there's only one George Osborne working there, but he seems incredulous that I'd be there to see him.

I tell him that's exactly who I'm here to see.

He calls up. I hear him say, "Annabel Port is here to see George Osborne." Then I get the phone passed to me. It's a strict-sounding lady, who tells me there is nothing in the diary.

"What's it regarding?" she asks.

"Well, I'm a tax collector and I've been dealing with Sir Philip Green and he's got some extra tax to be transferred to the Treasury."

"Well, George Osborne's not here, he's overseas," she snaps at me.

Maybe George and Philip are overseas together, talking about how flabbergasted they are that the super-rich are not paying enough tax. I'm not giving up though.

"Is there somebody else I could see?"

"No," is the blunt answer.

I lower my voice. "It's just that I've got this tax with me now."

She tells me it's more of a HMRC thing. I'm a little surprised that it's anyone's thing. But if there's somewhere better to go, I will go there. If I knew where it was.

"Remind me where HMRC is," I ask the strict lady.

I'm at another reception. I wonder if it's normal for tax collectors to spend this much time at receptions. I say, "Hello, I've been sent here by the Treasury. I'm a tax collector and I've got some extra tax that Sir Philip Green would like to transfer as a goodwill gesture."

"We just do meetings, not transfers," the woman says.

I feel like she's really saying, "This is not a bank, you idiot."

It has no effect on me though.

"It's just that I've come from a meeting at the Treasury."

This is in no way a lie. I really have come from a meeting at the Treasury. If you count standing at a reception as a meeting.

"Take a seat," she says to me briskly.

I do. It's a bit away from her desk so I can't hear what's going on but she appears to be making a lot of calls. Then two men with lanyards appear and start talking to the receptionist. One of them uses her phone to talk to someone.

I'm starting to feel a bit nervous. Then they're coming towards me.

One sits next to me and says, "So you've not got a meeting here, then?"

I explain the situation. He speaks to me in a very slow, gentle, kind and patient way. Almost like he would if he'd been told I'd had a breakdown but that the doctors were on the way and he just has to keep me calm. He's telling me I need to go on the website and sort things out from there.

"It's just that I've got it with me now," I tell him.

What harm can the two hangers, a highlighter pen and a blank BHS till roll do at this point? I start pulling them out of my bag.

He patiently looks at the hangers and the till roll. I can't find the highlighter pen. I make a great show of being very worried about this.

He's still telling me I need to go on the Internet.

Then he says gently, "We know you were trying to see the Chancellor."

I feel so embarrassed. The Treasury/HMRC grapevine has really sprung into action. I ask if I can leave the bits here. He says I can't. It's probably time to leave.

But I can still transfer the tax. I'll just put the two hangers, highlighter pen and BHS till roll in a Jiffy bag with a note for George Osborne. And if I can't find a pen, I'll cut out letters from a newspaper to spell out what I need to say. Then I'll pop it in the post. Super-rich Sir Philip Green has just paid a bit more tax.

26

The Challenge:
To befriend Vladimir Putin

How do you solve a problem like Putin? According to Geoff, befriend him. Maybe the Russian president has just been mixing with the wrong sort. Maybe he just needs a good friend to set him on the right track. A good friend like me. And there's only one way to make friends with someone quickly. Buy their friendship. If I give him a lovely gift, this friendship will be sorted.

I'm thinking about what he'd want, when I realise that people often give presents that they actually want themselves. So I look at what he's gifted in the past.

When Angela Merkel first visited him at the Kremlin, he bought her a fluffy toy dog. At first, this just seems like he bought her an idiotic present. That he thinks all grown women like cuddly toys. But actually it turns out Angela was bitten by a dog in the nineties and is really scared of them. It was actually a really evil present.

It could've been worse for Angela, though. He once gave Hugo Chavez a puppy. A gift that is a ten-to-fifteen-year daily responsibility. Hugo Chavez did die six months later, though. Still, it's nice that he spent the last months of his life scrubbing wee off the carpet.

Silvio Berlusconi got off lightly. Putin gave him a gift of a bed. That's an unusual gift. It's unlikely the recipient will go, "Oh just what I need, I haven't got a bed." But Putin clearly thinks it's a good present.

I call up a big department store and tell the main switchboard I want to know what bed is most popular with Russians.

"Let's have a look," he says.

This is exciting. Maybe they have a spreadsheet for things like this. But then he goes, "Okay, I'll put you through to the bed department."

I'm speaking to another man now and asking him what bed is most popular with Russians.

He repeats this back to me, then immediately adds, "I've not got a clue. We wouldn't know that. It's not something we'd be able to say."

"Oh," I say. "It's just that it's a gift for Vladimir Putin."

"Right, okay," he replies, like this is totally normal. To be buying a gift of a bed for Putin.

"Well, I can't really advise as it's down to individual preference as to mattress type and the decor of the bedroom."

"Well, which bed is most popular as a gift?"

"It's very rare for people to ask for beds as a gift. We don't get customers coming in saying I'm here to buy a gift for X, Y or Z."

I agree, that would be weird. To be buying a gift of a bed for a letter of the alphabet.

He goes on to say they recommend customers come in and try before they buy.

So I say, "What if I brought in Vladimir Putin?"

"Not an issue," he says. "Just let us know in advance what you'd require."

I think for a second and then ask, "Would you close the whole store for an hour on a Tuesday afternoon?"

The man says that although it's not his decision, he doesn't think that'd be possible. But perhaps Putin could come in early before they open.

Putin wouldn't be happy with that. But I'm sure there's a great bed for him there. I say, "Putin is a real manly man's man; have you got any beds with any really manly features?"

"Nothing at all," he says apologetically. "We do have some in dark colours and men do tend to go for those, but we don't have a manly bed like we do a boy's bed."

"What about a bed with pop-up nails that turn it into a bed of nails?"

"No, sorry, nothing like that."

I thank him and say I'll call back. I won't though as I've a better idea. A tank of piranhas! Putin would love that and better still, you can get one on eBay.

If this is not enough, if his friendship can't just be bought, another good basis for friendship is shared interests.

I know he loves judo. He released a learn judo DVD a few years back. I don't like judo, though. It annoys me that there are no proper fastenings on the jackets and they're always coming undone. When will they realise that a belt is not enough?

He's also into topless fishing. This is not for me. Ditto the topless horse riding. He likes deep-sea diving and went down into the ocean a few years back, where they'd planted some ancient pottery shards for him to amazingly find. But I don't like putting my head in the water.

Then I remember when he went in a motorised hang-glider to guide five cranes on their migration. I'm not sure why they needed his help. The idea of hang-gliding terrifies me, but I do like the idea of it feeling like flying.

I call up a place in the Midlands where you can do this. I say to the man, "Hi, I'm looking to book a session in a motorised hang-glider for Vladimir Putin, the Russian president."

"Right," he says in a completely disinterested tone. "We don't do motorised ones, just microlighting."

I ask him to explain the difference but don't retain any of the information. He does say it's the closest you can get to motorised hang-gliding though.

I ask, "Do you think Putin will like it?"

"Yes, it's good fun," he tells me. He's still disinterested.

I ask him if you do it with an instructor or solo. He tells me it's with an instructor. This is not good. Putin won't tolerate looking like he's not the boss.

"Could we make it look as if Putin was the instructor?" I ask.

"Yes, he could take over the controls at times, he can have as much or little control as he likes."

This is better. But I think it can get better still.

"What about making it a bit more macho, a bit more dangerous?"

He slightly more interested now. "Oh yes, he could do spirals."

"What about if Putin could find something up there?"

I'm thinking back to those ancient pottery shards he pretended to find underwater.

"Yes," he says. "They could do navigation."

"Oh no, I meant, could he find a new breed of bird or type of cloud or Amelia Earhart?"

The man says, "I suppose so. Not so much the birds. As we don't have many of them. But our instructors will know a lot about clouds."

He doesn't mention Amelia Earhart, so I leave that. I also don't mention this worrying news that they don't have many birds in the Midlands.

Instead I say, "One more thing, could he do it topless? Would that be an issue?"

"No, no, that's fine. Although he'll be cold."

I get the prices and it's cheaper than you'd think: £125 per hour. This is going to be a great bonding activity for Putin and me to do together.

I just need to get in touch with him now. I ring the Kremlin. Russia is four hours ahead so it's 7.30 p.m. there but they seem like hard workers, so I'm hopeful someone will answer. They don't. It just rings and rings. There's no answerphone, which is a bit weird. I try a twenty-four-hour helpline number that I've found on the Kremlin website. It's just a recorded message in Russian. I wait, hoping for an English version. But when it pauses and restarts again, it appears to be the same message. I can't know for sure, as I don't understand Russian, but I do feel like I'm listening to the distress signal recorded by Rousseau when she first got to the Lost island and transmitted from the radio tower on a loop.

Things are not going well, but I have a third option. There is a section on the Kremlin website where it says you can send

a letter to Putin, but over the Internet. So an email, really.
I send him this:

Dear Vladimir Putin,

I'm writing in the hope that we'll become friends. I
plan to send you a tank of piranhas as a token of my
affection (not a bribe), so could you let me have your
home address and I'll check the eBay seller delivers to
Russia?

I've also organised a bonding activity for us. To go
hang-gliding in the West Midlands (UK). I've already
checked that it's all right for you to do it topless and that
there's a good chance of discovering a brand-new type of
cloud so it should be a great day.

I don't know how many friends you've got already. If
it's not many, it might be because you're quite hard to get
hold of. Like when I googled the words "contact Putin",
I just got a lot of sites instructing me how to put in
contact lenses. Which was a bit annoying.

Regarding our communication as friends, I'm afraid
I can't speak Russian. But I do know how to say "my
knickers are red" in Polish, if that helps.

One big thing is I can't be friends with you if you're
homophobic. I know you've said recently you've
befriended some gay people. But the way you said this
felt a bit like the time my grandma (RIP) said to me, "The
doctor who saw me was black, but he was very good,"
and didn't realise that the "but" in this sentence was
problematic.

We've got to sort this out properly. Maybe you could

publicly French kiss Gorbachev. Or whatever the Russian version of French kissing is. This would send out a positive message.

Well, I do think we could be good friends. I know you're former KGB, but that doesn't faze me as my sister once tied me up and tickled me until I couldn't feel ticklish any more and I'm still not ticklish to this day.

So do get back to me.

SWALK

Annabel

I go to press send and suddenly get nervous as I really want to visit Russia one day. What if my name goes on a file now and when I enter the country I get thrown in a gulag?

I dismiss this fear and press send. Nothing happens. I keep pressing it again and again. What's worrying me more than it not sending is that it has been sending around about thirty times, and I'll look weird and obsessive. I'm not sure I could be friends with someone who sent their first email to me thirty times. If this doesn't work, if Putin and I don't become friends, at least now I know that this is the only reason.

27

The Challenge: To get an English Heritage blue plaque erected

I'd love a blue plaque on my house. Mainly as it would add value. You're not allowed to make any big changes once you've got this listed status, but I've not changed the horrible blinds that came with my house when I bought it three years ago, so I don't think any major alterations are going to happen. However, I'm pretty sure nobody famous has ever lived at my house, so I'll have to look elsewhere for the plaque.

When setting this challenge, Geoff suggested Guy Goma. I don't need any more encouragement. It was the eight-year anniversary last week of when Guy Goma was the wrong man interviewed on *BBC News 24*. Never forget. If you have forgotten or just have no idea who I mean, I urge you to immediately google him and watch the video. Then marvel at his chain of wonderful facial expressions.

He'd be perfect. I just need to do a bit of research to check he's a suitable candidate. English Heritage run the scheme and I learn on their website that in May 2010, after holding a two-day conference, they produced a guidance document. That sounds massively like an excuse for a drunken weekend away. I click on the document; it's 160 pages long. Even if the blue plaque was in my honour, I'm not sure I'd have the will to read it all. So I don't. I already feel like I know the important stuff.

I know they only pay for it if it's in London. That's fine. No problem there. There's a slight problem in that the subject of the plaque has to have been dead for a minimum of twenty years. But this is ridiculous. How can they get to enjoy it if they're not around? It's the same with saints. What's the point of becoming one when you're dead? When you can't use it to get restaurant reservations and plane upgrades?

This has to change. It would also be much more interesting if it's modern people. As soon as any celebrity moves out, they should put a plaque straight up and I feel that Guy Goma is the man to spearhead this change.

The only obstacle remaining is the question of where the plaque goes. My first thought is on the BBC building where the "Wrong Man" interview took place. I do slightly worry that maybe some fractionally more noteworthy things have happened at the BBC that might take precedence.

It could be Guy Goma's birthplace, but that's in the Republic of the Congo, which is outside of London so I'd have to pay for it myself. I next consider where he was living at the time of the interview. This would probably have been in London. It's impossible to find out where, though. It's impossible to find out anything about him as he's disappeared. Which explains why his biopic has not been made yet. They probably need him to sign some forms.

Then I remember that the reason Guy Goma was at the BBC was because he had a job interview. In fact, twenty minutes after being live on air, he went off and had the interview. He didn't get the job, unsurprisingly, as he'd found himself being interviewed on live television about something he knew nothing about TWENTY MINUTES beforehand. I'd love to see a video of this job interview. Anyway, this has given me an idea.

I call up the BBC's HR department and say, "I'm calling from English Heritage's blue plaques department and we're looking to celebrate the ten-year anniversary of Guy Goma's appearance on *BBC News 24* with a plaque on the house he lived in at the time. Obviously, we need his address from back then, though, so could you look it up for me?"

I get my pen ready to write down the details. However, the man says he can't give that information out over the phone because of data protection and that I have to email.

This is great. They can give me the address, just not over the phone.

He then says he'll speak to his line manager just to clarify the situation. I don't stop him as while I'm on hold I have a nice time imagining that conversation.

"Boss, I've got someone on the line who wants Guy Goma's address."

"Who's Guy Goma?"

"The wrong man on *BBC News 24*."

"What does she want his address for?"

"Um, she's from English Heritage and they're going to put a blue plaque on his house."

He comes back on the line and confirms that I need to

email in. I do. It's a bit unfortunate at this stage that I've said I'm from English Heritage as I don't have an English Heritage email address, but I manage to get round this by writing that I'm a freelancer working for English Heritage. I'm sure they have lots of freelancers doing all their dirty work.

I don't have to wait long for an email back from HR. It's just an automated one giving me my case reference number but I'm well on my way to getting a blue plaque up for Guy Goma.

What I need now is support from significant others. When I read about recent blue plaques on the English Heritage website, one name keeps coming up. They are always saying, "The blue plaque scheme is generously supported by David Pearl."

David Pearl, I discover, is a property developer on the *Sunday Times* Rich List. He's a real hotshot. I get straight on the phone to his company and ask to speak to him. Remarkably I get put through; I don't even have to say who I am. Unfortunately, it goes to voicemail. But the voicemail gives out his mobile number.

I'm very excited to have a hot-shot's mobile phone number. I immediately dial it but I get an answerphone again, so I leave a message, telling him I'm calling from English Heritage. Annoyingly, I keep saying "plaque" wrong so that it rhymes with "dark" and not "hack". I have to keep correcting myself, which I don't think looks very professional.

I don't hear back from him straight away so I decide that now would be a good point to stop and reflect on my progress so far. I make a list of what I've not yet achieved.

1. Any kind of address for Guy Goma to put the blue plaque up at.
2. Any form of support.

This is just two things, which is great. I make a list of what I have achieved.

1. Nothing.

This is not great, but there's still time and I've not even been in contact with English Heritage yet. That is what I'm going to do now and I've got an excellent plan involving the hotshot benefactor David Pearl.

The plan is, I go to the headquarters of English Heritage and get this Guy Goma plaque fast-tracked by pretending to be David Pearl's new executive assistant. "Pretending" is a good word as it's much nicer-sounding than "fraudulently imitating".

It's probably going to seem a bit weird that this executive assistant hasn't made an appointment, so I create an assistant who is very posh and brilliant but chaotic. A flawed genius. Her name is Angelica Princegood.

I head off to the offices. As I'm walking in to the reception, I put my phone to my ear.

"Yes, Mr Pearl, yes. Right, yes, of course," I say in my poshest voice.

There's somebody talking to the receptionist so I have to keep it up as I'm not sure she heard the first bit. I've kind of run out of things to say though. I find myself saying, "Three times three," "Yes, Zanzibar," "Eight o'clock, right, right, okay, okay."

In my head, David Pearl is a very demanding boss. As the other person at reception walks away, I finish with, "Okay, Mr Pearl, I'm here now, okay, David, bye."

Then I give the receptionist a big smile and introduce myself.

"Hi, I'm Angelica Princegood, David Pearl's new executive assistant. I just thought I'd come and introduce myself."

Before I'd arrived, I'd looked up a name of someone that worked there. I mention that now and say how I'd love to say hi to them.

It turns out this woman is on leave, but the receptionist, who is being really nice to me, says she'll call her replacement.

I take a seat and there's soon a smiling lady shaking my hand. I introduce myself again and ask if she's got a sec for me to tell her about something Mr Pearl is really keen on.

"Of course," she says.

I tell her it's about a blue plaque and Mr Pearl has got the suggestion of someone fabulous. She asks who.

"Guy Goma," I say.

"Right," she says. She sounds a little unsure.

"Do you know who that is?" I ask.

She doesn't, which probably explains why she's still sitting talking to me and smiling.

"He was the wrong man on *BBC News 24*. Isn't that fabulous?"

"Oh yes!" she cries. "Oh perfect!"

She is, without doubt, one of the politest people I've ever met. Or maybe funding at English Heritage is in a dire situation and if David Pearl suggested a blue plaque for that monkey in the sheepskin jacket in IKEA, they'd be equally enthused.

She's now asking questions about the house where the plaque would be put: "Does it have the original façade?" I have no idea, but I tell her it does and pray she doesn't ask me where it is.

She then tells me I've got to bear in mind it can take up to two years. This is probably as I'm getting a bit overexcited, which has the unfortunate side effect of my posh accent slipping a bit. But I tell her that's perfect, as in two years it's the ten-year anniversary of Guy being on *BBC News 24*.

"Oh, it couldn't be more perfect!" she agrees. She asks me a few more questions about Mr Pearl and whether he'd be involved in any publicity for this.

I imagine there are many more questions going through her mind. Like, for example, why is the executive assistant of someone on the *Sunday Times* Rich List wearing jeans, trainers and a T-shirt.

There are many questions going through my mind too. Like why am I pretending to be an executive assistant in order to get a blue plaque for Guy Goma?

"Well, great to get that sorted," I say. "I can't wait for all this to happen. Do please call David's office and keep us updated."

I leave them to find out Guy's address and make a confusing phone call to David Pearl. If they can get him to answer his phone. It's now surely just a matter of time before we'll all be making a pilgrimage to the Guy Goma blue plaque house. I'll be going all the way there on my knees.

28

The Challenge:
To become the new CEO of Tesco

The CEO of Tesco has been ousted and I see no reason at all why I can't replace him. I've shopped there loads of times. I've also worked in supermarkets before, stacking shelves and on the till, so I know what a supermarket needs. Yes, I've never managed anyone at all ever or done a spreadsheet or even know the basics about finances, sales, marketing, etc. But I know what makes a supermarket good. It's basically just food.

I've already got a lot of very strong opinions and I'm hoping lots of my ideas will inject new life into Tesco as they're doing pretty badly at the moment. I think only one in every seven pounds spent in the UK is being spent at Tesco.

My first idea is to change the name of Tesco Express. I've been to a Tesco Express several times and there is no Express involved. It's not in any way fast. You spend ages looking for some fairly basic products, limes or olives or pineapple juice, and they don't have it. So you have to go somewhere else.

It's not fast, it's small. They should never have got the two confused. I come up with a list of some new, more suitable names:

Tesco Mini
Tesco Diddy
Tesco Streamlined
Tesco Titchy
Tesco Okay If You Just Want Bread and Milk

To be honest, I'm not even sure about the Tesco bit when I learn how the name came about. Jack Cohen started the company on a market stall in the East End in 1919, which is how all supermarkets started, apart from Waitrose. I think. He sold a tea by T. E. Stockwell and took the TES then added the first two letters from his surname and got Tesco.

This is terrible. What if the tea had been by C. H. Irving? He'd have had to call his supermarket Chico. Or if the tea had been by D. I. Smith, it would've been Disco. Actually, that would've been brilliant.

I decide to leave the Tesco bit for now, though, as there are probably more important things. Like the most annoying thing about supermarkets of today: the self-service checkouts with their "unexpected item in bagging area". There's nothing I can do about this happening, as the technology is just not quite there yet. But I can make it less annoying. For example:

"Are you trying to steal something?"

"Are you trying to do an Antony Worrall Thompson?"

"UH-UH", like the *Family Fortunes* incorrect buzzer.

"The technology's not quite there yet, sorry."

Any of these are better.

Another area I want to get involved in is trollies and baskets. Using a trolley is one of the few times in life that I feel like a grown-up. The only other times are when I'm writing on a whiteboard and writing a cheque. I feel masterful and in charge when I'm pushing a trolley. But I'm often not buying enough to warrant using one. So I use a basket. But what if there was a hybrid of the trolley and basket? A trasket. A mini-trolley, similar to what they sometimes have for kids to push around, but adult-sized.

Also, as I quite often leave my basket somewhere and wander off and then can't find it again, I suggest a remote-controlled flare on the trasket, which you activate when lost.

Next, the Clubcard. I've got nothing against something that saves you money. Even though I know it's really to keep tabs on you and they probably sell the information to the FBI. But I want the card to be exciting, like the American Express Centurion card, Nandos black card or your National Insurance card when you get it at sixteen.

The answer is obvious. You start with a Tesco Value card, then move up to an ordinary Tesco card. Then for the elite customer, the Tesco Finest card, which will be silver. It doesn't exist yet and it's already the thing I want most in the world. Apart from a trasket.

It won't just be for rich people, though, which is good as then I'd never get it. It won't just reward money spent, it will reward loyalty. So every time you shop you get points but if you go to Sainsbury's, you'd get some deducted. I'm not sure how this will work but I'll leave the logistics to someone else.

There will be great rewards for the Finest card as well, not just money-off vouchers. There'll be benefits similar to the

Blue Peter badge. Like free visits to the Imperial Leather soap factory. And the front seats on the top deck of a bus will be reserved for Tesco Finest Clubcard holders.

I'm pretty much finished now, just a few more small things to add, which are: bring back display pyramids of stuff like baked beans, games of hide and seek in store that you can join in with, everyone's allowed to lick the cake-mix bowl in the bakery bit and write on all the banana skins. And they should stock some random items from other supermarkets, like Sainsbury's tinned tomatoes, to confuse shoppers.

If only the outgoing CEO had had all these ideas. It might have been very different for him. Retail glory awaits me now though. Right after I've gone out in the field to test my ideas.

I go to a Tesco. A Tesco Metro. I think these are just a slightly bigger Tesco Express, but I don't know as nobody really knows. As soon as I get there, I know what I want to test first. The trasket. The basket/trolley hybrid. I do notice that they have those baskets you drag along behind you like wheelie suitcases. I can't stress enough that this is not what I mean and does not in any way fulfil my requirements. I like the feeling of pushing a trolley. I don't want to do dragging and bending down to put stuff in the basket.

I have a little wander around and see one of those metal shelves on wheels that the shelf stackers use to move stock around. It's not a really tall one; it's about waist height with a tray of potatoes on it. It's calling out to be converted into a trasket. Begging me.

I find a man who is replenishing the sandwiches and ask him if I can put my basket on top of the shelves on wheels and use it.

Before I've even finished asking, he's lifting the potatoes off and saying, "Yeah, sure." I make a mental note to give him a promotion once I'm CEO. Then I put my basket on top.

"Why don't you get a trolley though?" he asks.

I tell him, "This feels better to me."

"Okay, sure," he says. And I mentally give him a pay rise too.

I'm pushing around my trasket, my basket on the shelves on wheels, and getting a few envious looks from fellow customers. I think it was envy even though it was not dissimilar to the looks I got the time my flip-flop broke on the Tube and I walked barefoot down Oxford Street to the nearest shoe shop.

The only thing missing is the remote-controlled flare but I'd googled how to make a flare and you needed potassium nitrate and they don't sell that here since it's only a Tesco Metro.

It's now time to concentrate on the pyramid of items. I really miss the big pyramid of tins in supermarkets. I see the man who let me make my trasket and possibly now regrets it and say, "Hey, why don't you have pyramids of tins?"

"Oh," he says, then "hold on", and goes off, I presume to hide in the staffroom toilets, but he comes back with the duty manager.

I tell him my idea. He seems keen but says, "Well, our special offer at the moment for Belvita biscuits is coming to an end." This doesn't seem in any way related to what I've just suggested. We are by the Belvita biscuits though, so I take three boxes and form a pyramid with them on the floor.

"It's a bit small," he says. He's got a point.

I say, "Yeah, but let's leave it."

He tells me he can't leave it on the floor. I'm worried he's not getting the whole pyramid thing. The base has got to go on the floor.

I move on to another idea. "Why don't you have games of hide and seek in store?"

"Oh," he says. "We've been thinking of activities to make the store a bit more fun."

He really says that.

"Do it!" I encourage him. He does seem very keen, so I'm very pleased with the feedback for that idea.

I feel like I should buy something now so I see some biscuits I've not had for ages, Toffypops, and take them to the self-service till. When I get there, I get very, very lucky. As there is a man there fixing one. It's all lifted up and I can see the wires underneath. I've never seen one being fixed before. This is perfect. This man must be an expert who can make all kinds of adjustments.

"Hi, could you change that bit that says 'unexpected item in bagging area'? It's really annoying. You could change it to 'are you stealing something?' or 'UH-UH.'" I make the *Family Fortunes* buzzer sound loudly.

"Impossible," he says. I'm pretty sure it's not impossible. I don't say that, though. I say, "I could voice it for you now." He shakes his head. He's not so friendly. I leave it because I don't want to cause a scene. Everyone else here is so nice and I'll be telling the board this when I meet with them to secure the job.

I do some research as to who is on the board and make an unpleasant discovery. They already have a new CEO. He started on Monday. This is a big worry, but if I could discredit him somehow, they could get rid of him at the end of his probation period.

I call up head office. A lady answers. I tell her I've got some information on the new CEO, Dave Lewis, and ask if she's got pen and paper. She says a very unsure, "Okay."

"The thing is," I tell her, "I saw him shopping in Waitrose."

She repeats it back to me in the writing-something-down voice, "shopping in Waitrose".

I ask her to pass it on and hang up. Then I call straight back. Someone different answers the phone but I use a different voice. I do my man voice.

"Hello," I say in my deepest tone. "I've got something I need to tell you about the CEO, Mr Lewis."

There's a long silence. Eventually she says, "I'm not sure who you need to speak to, would it be a complaint?"

"How about I'll tell you and you pass it on?" I suggest. She agrees a bit reluctantly.

I tell her, "Well I saw the CEO in Tesco at a self-service till and he got frustrated with it and gave it a little kick."

She laughs. I'm concerned she's not taking this seriously. "I'll leave that with you, then," I say and hang up.

I call back again. It's yet another different person but I still use another voice. I don't want them to think it's a vendetta from one person. I'm sure they'll think nothing of how the calls all came one after the other. From the same number.

This time I use my American voice and say, "I saw Dave Lewis dumping a Tesco trolley and not even near a store."

"Hold the line, please," she says and then I'm put through to customer services. I'm sure this isn't right at all, but I repeat my claim of the trolley-dumping.

"And where was this?" she asks.

I grab a place name out of the air, "Mile End." Then add, "By the canal." This seems realistic.

"And what exactly happened?" she asks. "Was he walking along or was the trolley dumped out of a car?"

The car-dumping story is very appealing but feels less realistic to me. Who is dumping trollies out of cars? I want to discredit this CEO, but I don't want to make him look like an animal. I tell her he was walking along.

"Okay, thank you," she says. The conversation is over. I hang up and call head office again. This time I use my posh voice.

"Oh, hello. I was in a Tesco, behind Dave Lewis in the basket queue. It was one of the ten items or less ones and his basket looked rather full, so I counted the items and there were twelve."

She says nothing and again I'm transferred to customer services. I'm starting to realise that customer services are the dumping ground for any calls other departments don't want to deal with.

I tell the new lady about the basket situation. When I'm finished she says, "I'm so sorry. Which store was it?" I tell her Bromley-by-Bow and hear typing noises. She's typing it up. Probably into a report for the board.

"And was it today?" she asks. I tell her it was.

"Did you continue to stay in the queue?"

"Yes," I say, "I just bit my tongue."

"And do you remember the checkout number?"

Who remembers this? I tell her I don't know. Then she wants me to describe the cashier so I say I can't remember faces.

"Well, I can empathise with you," she says. "The rule is difficult to impose. I can appreciate how frustrating this was for you and am very sorry for any delay you experienced."

She's clearly been well trained but this is not going to plan. I don't want to get a cashier in trouble. I say, "The point is, though, it was your CEO with too many items. He should know better."

"Could you hold the line?" she asks me now.

I'm on hold for so long I actually have to give up and hang up. I had planned to call back, accusing the CEO of using the magazine aisle like a library, not putting the checkout divider down for the next customer and eating an unpaid-for cherry tomato in store, but I feel like my job has more than been done.

He's been completely discredited. I just need to wait for his probation period to end and that job is mine. I can't wait to use a trasket.

29

The Challenge: To overthrow
something or someone

This is how this challenge was set on the radio show.

> Geoff: "I was thinking that you could start some kind of
> uprising and revolution and overthrow somebody."
> Me: "When you say you were thinking, how long were
> you thinking about it for, just out of interest?"
> Geoff: "Let me just check how long that Bruce
> Springsteen record was just now. Okay, four minutes and
> two seconds."
> Me: "Oh that long, wow!"
> Geoff: "Not all of it though, as I was on Facebook for
> some of it. And I'd found a weird skin tag under my
> armpit, which I was playing with for a while as well."

The conclusion was that he'd put around thirty seconds of
thought into this. I put around double that into deciding who
to overthrow.

I consider the government. The pros are: it's very fashionable at the moment to overthrow a government. The cons are: it would be a massive effort and I don't want to have effigies burnt of me for the next 400 years should I fail.

I consider the monarchy. The pros are: I get to live in Buckingham Palace. The cons are: bad décor and too much Tupperware.

I go through other British institutions: the NHS, BBC, armed forces, fish and chip shops, Marks & Spencer, the pub, the Post Office, Alan Bennett.

Looking down the list, I realise I quite fancy overthrowing a pub. Mostly as I like the idea of ringing the last orders bell and I'm sure there have been coups staged for lesser reasons.

It's probably better to go for a chain as I can take one and then the rest will topple. Much like Hitler's plans with Poland.

I pick a chain pub. Actually, it's less a traditional pub and more of a bar that also does food all day. I used to work in one of the branches so I've already got experience. I won't feel too much like the newbie revolutionary overthrower on my first day.

I make my way to a branch in London and walk in, trying to exude authority. It's hard when you're in jeans and a grey duffle coat.

But it's time to take control. I go to the bar, where I see two newspapers. They've just been casually placed there. I catch the eye of a barmaid.

"Hi. Annabel. Head office," I say briskly. "These newspapers are a bit messy. Could you put them so they fan out?"

"Oh, okay," she says but doesn't do anything. I show her what I mean.

She walks off, saying, "It's just that customers will keep moving them."

I'm briefly annoyed that she's answering back and making excuses until I remember that I'm not actually from head office.

I move down the bar to another barmaid. There's a very small liquid spillage about the size of a 50p.

"Hi. Annabel. Head office. Could you just mop up that spillage please?"

She does so straight away. I'm getting a taste for this now. I add, "And those brandy bottles behind you, can you straighten them out? They're lined up a bit wonky."

She does so with a smile.

I walk around now, inspecting the premises. It's fairly full; most tables are taken. I approach four people eating and ask, "How are you enjoying your food?"

The tell me it's all fine. I feel pleased that my pub is doing so well. I take some empty glasses to the bar and tidy some menus up. Then I approach two men in suits. They're just finishing their meal. I introduce myself as Annabel from head office and ask how their meal was.

"Great," they tell me.

There's now a slightly awkward pause so I blurt out, "And would you like a couple of coffees now on the house?"

They seem surprised and pleased. They would very much like a couple of coffees on the house.

I go to the bar and say to a barman, "Hi. Annabel. Head office. Could you just get me a couple of coffees on the house for those gentleman over there?" I point out the men in suits.

He nods and smiles. I'm not sure if this is a yes. I carry on with my inspection and after a short time I notice that some-body is taking two coffees over. I see there is some discussion, though, and then the two coffees are taken away.

I go over to the two men and ask, "Is everything okay?"

They look a bit embarrassed. I assure them the coffees are on the house.

"Oh, we're having them," one of the men says. "It's just that we changed the filter coffees for lattes."

I'm so in charge, I've just given two men some free posh coffees.

I'm a fairly rubbish revolutionary, though. I'm filled with fear that I'll be found out. I do the sensible thing. And leave. And practically run down the street.

This was a great start to my overthrowing career. I've got a real taste for being a rebel dictator. What next? I find myself thinking back to the royals and I realise I don't have to overthrow them all. I could just do one of them. Like Prince Andrew. And I know exactly where he's going to be today. The Big Bang Science Fair at the ExCel Centre in London. He's going to be there in his capacity as patron of the Young Engineers. I'm sure he's a great patron for these engineers, and they wouldn't rather have James Dyson, for example.

The only thing I don't know is what time he'll be there. I ring Prince Andrew's office and say to the lady, "Hello, I'm calling from the Big Bang Fair at ExCeL and was wondering what time Prince Andrew plans to come down today."

She asks me for my full name and then my telephone number. And then asks, "Are you running this visit at this event then?"

"No," I say. I can't lie.

"What's your position?"

"I'm head of the East London Prince Andrew Fan Club."

It turns out I can lie.

There's a silence, then she says, "Okay, let me get back to you."

But she doesn't. I decide just to go down there and hope for the best. I arrive around 1 p.m. I go to the registration booth and say to the woman there, "I'm here to take the place of Prince Andrew as the patron of Young Engineers."

"Oh, okay," she says.

Great! I'm here first. I can take his place and the overthrowing is complete.

She takes my name and goes off looking for my name card and lanyard. I'm so hoping to get the Prince Andrew one. I don't and, unsurprisingly, she can't find an Annabel Port name card.

"But not to worry," she says. "I'll make you one."

I'm not really sure what to do now. So I ask, "And what plans did you have for Prince Andrew?"

She doesn't know but she's going to ask the event organiser, Jeremy. I see her speaking to another lady in the booth who then comes over to check my details. I confirm with her that I am here to take the place of Prince Andrew.

She goes on her walkie-talkie and I hear her say, "I'm here with Annabel Port and she's come instead of Prince Andrew."

Then she tells me Jeremy is coming, but the ExCel is so large I might have a bit of a wait. It's interesting that nobody seems that fussed that the Queen's son has been replaced by a nobody. In fact, they are all being lovely to me. Perhaps they're even relieved it's me. I might go round everywhere saying I've turned up in his place.

I'm waiting for a long time though. So long that I'm starting to lose my bottle and worry about what I'll do if Prince Andrew turns up now.

Eventually Jeremy appears and I have to explain why I'm here again.

"Oh," he says when I've finished. "It's just that the prince was here this morning."

This is disastrous. I'm about to be exposed as a liar. There's only one thing I can do. Keep lying. I say, "Yes, he wanted me to come in his place for the second session."

I don't even really know what I mean by second session. Or why in my fantasy world Prince Andrew would ask me to do this.

"Okay," he says. "I'll speak to the person in charge of the visit." He goes on his walkie-talkie. "I've got someone here from the Duke of York's office – could you come down to speak to her?"

There are now two paths ahead of me. One where I'm humiliated and exposed as a fraud. And one where I have to spend the rest of the afternoon being shown around a science fair. I honestly don't know which is worse.

But then I realise there is another path. I take out my mobile and tell Jeremy I'll make a call to double check there's not been a mix-up. I press my phone to my ear then slowly start edging towards to the door.

I make a face as if to say the mobile-phone reception is not great, so I'd better step outside. I go out the exit and even though it's through a huge glass wall, without looking back I immediately run all the way to the train station.

So I've overthrown a bar (kind of), and Prince Andrew (not at all) but now I want to aim even higher. A big international company.

The very first one I think of is Saatchi & Saatchi. I'm not sure why that was my first thought. Maybe because as a big media company, it's not completely unfamiliar to me. Or perhaps it's because I like the idea of changing the company name to Port & Port.

I begin by looking for the name of someone very high up the food chain. I find one for the chief financial officer. This is where I'll start the overthrow. Once I've got control of the money, I've got control of it all. And can pay myself billions.

The plan is, I'll go to their reception, say I've got a meeting with this chap and then once he comes down, take it from there.

I'm not optimistic. At my work, I couldn't be further from chief financial officer in terms of importance and I wouldn't come down to reception if a stranger turned up claiming to have a meeting with me.

But, as I get to the top of the steps to the door, I look down and engraved into the stone are the words, "Nothing is Impossible."

This gives me a real boost. I walk in to the reception and say, "Hi, I'm here for a meeting with Dan, the chief financial officer. It's Annabel Port."

She tells me to take a seat and I hear her call up.

What should happen now is that she calls me back over and tells me that no such meeting is scheduled and after me attempting some other equally pathetic ways to get in, I leave.

This doesn't happen. She doesn't say anything to me. And

after a short time, a man is walking towards me and saying, "Annabel, hi!" and shaking my hand.

It is the chief financial officer. This is very unexpected but it's my big chance and I might not have long, so I get straight to the point and say, "Hello, I've got some bad news, I'm afraid: I've come to take over your job."

He does a nervous, uncomfortable laugh and replies, "Right, where do you want to start?"

I'm quite confused by this reaction but say, "Well, why don't you show me your office so I can get started?"

"Okay," he agrees and leads me through a door and then down a long corridor. "It's like a maze in here," he says.

It's not. It's just a long, L-shaped corridor, but I go, "Isn't it?"

We then go through an open-plan office into his own private office.

I cannot quite believe this is happening. Why is the chief financial officer of Saatchi & Saatchi, a global advertising company, taking me, a complete stranger who has just declared an interest in taking over his job, into his office?

He closes the door and tells me to take a seat.

"Shall I sit behind your desk, so I can get used to it?" I ask.

"Okay," he says. Then adds, "Actually you'd better not as you'll see things you're not supposed to."

We sit down at a round table in his room. He seems a little bit flustered.

"Okay, sorry, I did have this in the diary but I've not had a chance to prepare."

This is even more confusing. Who has an overthrow in their diary?

"You had this in the diary?" I ask.

"Yes, GEP," he says. "You are from GEP?"

"No. I'm just here to take over."

He is very confused. And maybe slightly scared. "Sorry, who are you?" he asks.

"I'm an overthrower," I tell him proudly.

It transpires I've turned up at the exact time that he was due to have a meeting with someone. But, amazingly, he doesn't demand that I leave immediately. He's probably still in shock from having the world's weirdest meeting.

And I'm not giving up. I ask about his staff. "Will I get on well with them?"

He doesn't seem that keen on answering my question so I ask, "Do you not want me to take over your job?"

He tells me that his family like him earning money. I want to suggest he send his kids up chimneys, but it's a credit to me that I don't. Instead I generously tell him that he can work under me for the same wages. I don't know if this is possible, but I want to get him on side.

He says it's not really his decision. He's still not told me to leave. This is the politest man ever. He's so nice that I eventually I say, "Shall I go now?"

He is a little busy, as it turns out. And he's so nice that he really apologises to me and even suggests another company for me to try and take over. I hope none of this stemmed from fear.

But I do feel that for a short while this afternoon, I managed to overthrow the financial department of a global company. If you really, really stretch the definition of "overthrow".

30

The Challenge: To create a rival
to the Tour de France

The Tour de France is by far the most famous cycling race, in that I can't even name another one. They've got the whole fast-cycling thing pretty sewn up. But there's no reason why I can't create another kind of race that is as good. Or better. I look to see how the Tour de France started so I can steal ideas for starting my own.

It is not at all what I expected. It started solely as a way of trying to increase sales of a French sporting magazine. It was 1903, sales were bad, and their rival was way ahead. So they had a meeting to discuss what to do and at the very last moment the most junior member of staff suggested a bike race across France. The editor welcomed any increase in the popularity of cycling as he also owned a velodrome, and so the Tour de France was born.

It's now obvious what I've got to do. Find a struggling

magazine, invent a race that somehow benefits them, and then I've got a big hit on my hands.

I get to work finding the right magazine, thinking it shouldn't be too hard as aren't all magazines struggling? I look down a long list and one catches my eye. It's called *Canal Boat*. An idea is starting to form.

Their monthly circulation figures are 9,995, which I'd classify as struggling. No offence, *Canal Boat*.

Better still, it has a rival, *Waterways World* magazine, which sells a slightly more impressive 11,559 a month. Making it Britain's best-selling canal magazine. But not for long. Not after *Canal Boat* magazine become the official sponsors of my race and get all the exclusive insider news and interviews. Sales will go through the roof. As long as it is a really low roof, like they had in medieval times.

I've just got to invent the race now. The obvious route would be along the canal network of the UK. I don't waste any time thinking of a non-obvious one. This is perfect, as it has the benefit of going all over the UK, so no one feels left out.

I draw the line at racing in canal boats, though. They are far too slow and I'm pretty sure there'd not be enough room for all the thousands of competitors to overtake.

There are loads of other, way better water vehicles. Like the banana boat, rubber ring, punt, jet ski, gondola and dinghy. Each stage could use a different one, which immediately improves upon the Tour de France, with it's boring bikes-only rule.

I'm really warming to the idea now, and also decide to add in obstacles to make it more thrilling. There could be an up-ended shopping trolley, hypodermic needles and a dead body. Probably a fake one that looks like Dirty Den, rather than a real one.

The great thing is that the UK was the first country to have a nationwide canal network, so it's really celebrating that. And there's also scope to do sections of the race abroad like the Tour de France does. My race could go to Venice and Panama.

I just need to call *Canal Boat* magazine to get confirmation they're interested. Obviously, they will be. I'm very excited. I feel a lot like that person who rang up a shampoo company and said he could double their profits with just three words: "rinse then repeat". I'm not 100% sure this is true, but anyway, I'm excited.

I quickly check how much the sales of the 1900s French sporting magazine went up after the Tour de France. It was 160%. I'm verging on giddy as I dial the number. It connects, it rings and then just keeps on ringing. I keep trying. Nothing. I'm starting to understand why *Canal Boat* is not the number-one canal magazine.

I've got no choice. I don't like doing it but I've got to go to their big rival. The number-one canal magazine, *Waterways World*. They might be doing pretty well in the canal publication world but there's always room for improvement. I call them up and get put straight through to the editor. This is why they are number one.

"Hello," I say. "I know how I can increase your profits by 160%."

He laughs and says he admires my optimism. Then concedes, "Okay, I'm interested. How?"

I tell him. I give him a brief history of how the Tour de France increased sales of a French sporting magazine by 160% and how I plan to set up my own version of the race along canals to do the same for his magazine. But instead of bikes, it'd be with vehicles like the banana boat, rubber ring, punt, jet ski, gondola, dingy, lilo and bits of floating wood like you get after a shipwreck.

When I've finished, he responds with, "Well, that was an excellent pitch."

I know from watching *The Apprentice* that it's not easy to do a pitch, so I'm very happy.

He asks what organisation I'm from. I tell him I'm doing it independently. To his credit, he doesn't immediately put the phone down. Instead he asks about my involvement in the waterways world.

"I went on a canal boat last Thursday evening," I tell him. Which I really did. That was a stroke of luck. I sound very experienced now.

I do worry it's all sounding a little bit weird, so I distract him by saying that I really want him to beat *Canal Boat* and *Towpath Tales* magazines by one hundred times. And don't mention that I'd spent all afternoon trying to get hold of *Canal Boat* magazine first.

He asks what happens now. I say, "Well I'm going to be meeting with the Minister for Culture and Sport." This is not strictly a lie as I do plan to meet with them.

I think he might be a bit impressed by this. I've won him back and he's now saying it fits in well with the Canal Trust as they're hoping to attract more young people to the waterways.

I think there already are a lot of young people on the waterways. They're mainly taking drugs, but they are still young. I don't mention this though.

As he's now asking how old I am. I tell him thirty-nine. It's a bit embarrassing. I think maybe he thought I was a lot younger. But he's polite and says, "Oh right, yes, well, do email me."

I do, and then make preparations for my meeting with the Minister for Culture and Sport. By looking up their name. It's Sajid Javid, who is fairly new in the job. This is perfect as he might not know all the ropes yet and think it's perfectly normal to speak to me. I also remember that he recently went with George Osborne to Pinewood Studios to visit the *Star Wars* set and he said, "The force is clearly strong here." So I know he loves a little joke. This gives me an idea to make him warm to me. I'll litter our conversation with puns.

I spend some time preparing these and then call up the Department for Culture and Sport and ask to speak to Sajid Javid. The receptionist asks what it's regarding.

"The rival to the Tour de France," I tell her.

"And have you previously been in contact?"

"Oh yes," I lie.

She puts me through and there's a man's voice on the line.

"Hello, Sajid?" I say.

"No, it's his office," the man's voice replies.

This is not ideal but at least I'm speaking to someone. I explain to him all about my rival to the Tour de France. He's very serious and grown-up sounding, but I tell him about the pedalos, lilos and gondolas with confidence.

As I'm finishing, I'm thinking, maybe to seal the deal I can throw in some of the puns I came up with. Maybe it's not just Sajid, maybe the whole office loves a little joke. I end my pitch with, "So waterway to celebrate the UK canal network."

He ignores this masterful use of language and asks, "Well, what do you want from us?"

It is an excellent question and not one that I'd considered.

Why am I ringing the Department for Culture and Sport?

"Erm, your authorisation," I say.

He says briskly, "What do you mean?"

"Well . . ." I falter a bit here while my brain scrambles to find an answer to this question. Then I blurt out, "It's going to be massive, like the Olympics, so obviously we need your support."

He tells me to email and when telling me the email address he spells out the word "office". He thinks I'm the kind of person that can't spell the word "office".

I won't be deterred though. I email explaining it all again, including *Waterways World* and the banana boats, etc. Then as I'm really hoping Sajid will see this email, now is my big chance to use all my puns. I continue with:

Ours was the first country to have a nationwide canal network. "Waterway" to celebrate this. This new race will be a great way "towpath" the time. Don't put a "lock" on this idea. The future is looking "Rosie, Jim".

If only his name was Jim. That last one would've worked a lot better. I think it says a lot about me that I used it anyway. Sadly I wasn't able to use the pun I'd created for if he was waffling on a bit on the phone, which was, "Sorry, can I just 'barge' in here and interrupt you?"

Now, somewhat surprisingly, I don't hear back immediately or even that day or ever, actually. Maybe they laughed so much at the puns that they forgot to reply. So I've left it all in the safe hands of *Waterways World*, while I work on picking up some speed on a lilo.

31

The Challenge:
To become a self-help guru

I am very keen on becoming a self-help guru, from the moment I find out it's a $10 billion industry. An industry where one of the most popular books is about how if you think about something hard enough it will come to you. This book, *The Secret*, has sold 19 million copies and made $300 million. Not such a secret any more, really. A secret that 19 million know. But it's no wonder that others have tried to cash in on this industry.

One that catches my eye is by Larry Winget and called *Shut Up, Stop Whining and Get a Life: A Kick-Butt Approach To A Better Life*. That's his most successful one. There are several follow-ups. How he had the material to fill one book is a mystery, but sequels include: *Your Kids Are Your Own Fault, You're Broke Because You Want To Be, Grow A Pair, It's Called Work For A Reason* and *No Time for Tact*. I'm a little bit worried that this man is actually just rude.

I also really like a book by Hiroyuki Nishigaki called *How to Good-Bye Depression*. Not "how to say goodbye", but "how to good-bye depression". Like good-bye is a verb.

You're probably now thinking, *Stop going on about grammar, tell us how to goodbye depression, how does the book say to do it?*

The answer is, constrict the anus 100 consecutive times a day and dent the navel 100 times a day. I try it. I manage eight anus constrictions before I start feeling a bit disturbed and no navel dents as I don't understand how to dent my navel. I do feel slightly happier afterwards. But only because it's over and I've promised myself I'll never knowingly constrict my anus again.

All this is giving me a lot of ideas though. Three, in fact. Which is probably two more than any other self-help book by the sounds of things, so I'm pleased with my progress and already mentally spending my $300 million.

Firstly, I was thinking about what I want to learn from a self-help book. And I realise that what I want is to get all my desires with minimal effort. Preferably no effort at all.

And it comes to me. What I want is to improve my life while I'm asleep. And I know how. This is the first excerpt from my book:

Most of us just fall asleep in any old position without thinking of the consequences. About how it will affect our waking lives. Imagine a bit of paper screwed up in a ball overnight. Then it being unscrewed in the morning. It's going to be really creased, isn't it? All the pristine bits of paper will be staring at its creases and judging it. This will affect its self-esteem and then how it does its job, interacts with friends and behaves with its love partner. Think of yourself as that bit of paper when you lie in bed at night and don't curl up in a ball. Stretch out as far as you can all night. Do this and I guarantee the next day you will be more successful in everything you do. This is because science dictates that if your blood can flow through your body all night without any restriction (i.e., a bent limb) your brain power will be increased by 10% and other things like energy, dedication and likeability are increased by 15%.

I think you'll agree it's got everything. Made-up science, the promise of becoming a better person. Everything.

I move on to the second part now. The reason why things like *The Secret* are so popular is because we love the idea that you just ask for something and you get it. The second part is heavily based on this.

Here it is:

If you really want something, don't worry about working hard to achieve it. Why waste your time? Think about what you want. For example, I want to win the lottery, or I want a perfect boyfriend or I want straighter legs. Then all you have to do is shout it out as loud as you can in front of as many people as possible, e.g., a packed train carriage or a full cinema. It's important that as many people as possible hear it, as science dictates that if your desires are registered in multiple brains, the electrical activity creates the energy that allows your desires to be fulfilled.

I just need to write the third part now, which will be inspirational quotes that I live by. These are:

1. That lyric from "Girls Just Want to Have Fun" about

some guy hiding a girl away from the world but she
wants to be the one to walk in the sun.
2. Keep on keeping on.
3. It is what it is.

I feel I've got myself a very promising self-help book so far.

The one thing I feel I'm missing, though, is a big celebrity
supporter, and I know exactly who I want. Noel Edmonds.
When he returned to television, after a long break, with *Deal
or No Deal*, he attributed it to "Cosmic Ordering". The idea
that you ask the cosmos for something and then get it. So,
rather than world peace or the eradication of all diseases, he
got himself a teatime game show. No judgement, Noel.

I'm sure nobody would know about the Cosmic Ordering
Service if not for him. He'd be perfect. I find out the email
address of his manager and send this:

Dear John,

    I am an exciting new self-help guru, and my book
*Make All Your Dreams Come True with Zero Effort Apart from
Buying and Then Reading This Book but It's an Easy Read So
Don't Worry* is about to be published.

    I know Noel has been supportive of the Cosmic
Ordering Service as he asked the Cosmos for a
nice house and teatime quiz show and got both. So I
wondered if he'd like to read my book and see if any
more of his dreams come true. Maybe he wants another
TV show, as to be honest I used to be mad on *Deal or
No Deal* but on the rare occasions I turn it on now he's
wearing a lady's bonnet or something to liven it up, and
that does worry me.

    I've been a big fan of Noel going back to the *Swap*

Shop days so it would be a real honour to have him read
my book and an even bigger honour if he gave it the
thumbs up.

    Let me know if he's keen and then I'll forward you
three significant chapters.

    Many thanks and all best wishes,
      Annabel
      Guru

I don't have to wait long at all to hear back. His manager
thanks me for my email and the offer, but as Noel has got
a new book coming out soon, "He doesn't feel it would be
appropriate to read your book at the moment."

I'm not entirely sure what this means. Is Noel worried that
he might accidentally steal some of my ideas for his book? Or
do authors not read other books when they've got their own
coming out as it's like sleeping with the enemy? This is a real
worry for me. I love reading, so I'm not sure I want to give
that up when my self-help book comes out.

Or perhaps it was a very polite way of saying no. But the
most interesting thing he says is "new book". Noel's got an
old book? I go straight on Amazon. And he does. In 2007, he
published, *Positively Happy, Cosmic Ways to Change your Life*.

And in 1994, *Hold Your Own House Party*, featuring Noel
on the cover in a dinner suit and holding a candelabra above
a laden table. There's a new copy on sale for £2,499.50. I can
definitely afford that once my book takes off.

Anyway, I say all this to distract you from the fact that
finding a celebrity supporter hasn't gone massively well. But
that's okay as I probably need to focus more on the actual book.
And one thing is missing. While there's lots of science, there's

not much in the way of scientific evidence for my claims.

I decide to go out to Piccadilly Circus to test them out. I approach a man, a builder, and say, "Hello, I'm Annabel, a self-help guru. Would you like me to make your dreams come true?"

It's only as I say it that I realise it sounds a bit dodgy but the man says, "No I'm all right, thanks."

I try someone else, a man in a T-shirt with the words "the spirit of rock". His response is, "No, sorry," like he's inconveniencing me by not letting me make his dreams come true.

A girl in a shirt with elephants on says, "No, it's okay."

The next person completely ignores me. What is wrong with people?

Then I try a tall man with a beard. He says, "Well, that's lovely of you. Tell me more."

I do. I explain the sleeping technique and the shouting technique. He listens and nods. Then says, "It's funny, as I do something similar to you."

It turns out he's a life coach who works with men. In particular, how to talk to women. I don't ask any more questions about this for fear he's a British Julien Blanc and runs courses with titles like "Make girls beg to sleep with you after short-circuiting their emotional and logical mind". Instead I ask him if he wants to try out the shouting your dream thing. He tells me he doesn't as he's tired and he's relaxing now.

I make a mental note to add to my self-help book, "Don't relax at Piccadilly Circus; it's not very relaxing there."

The man asks me if anyone has done the shouting technique. I feel a bit embarrassed that nobody has, so I say, "Yes, I'm going to do it now."

It probably would've been less embarrassing to admit nobody had ever done it than shout my dream out at Piccadilly Circus.

But, anyway, I do. I shout out my biggest desire.

"I REALLY WANT MY SELF-HELP BOOK TO BE A BIG SUCCESS!"

Only one person looked, which says a lot about London.

But the good news is, now that I've done that, it will come true. I'm not worried at all about my book. It's time to start thinking about other ways that self-help gurus make money. And make no mistake about it, that's what I'm interested in.

I google "the richest self-help guru" and the name Tony Robbins comes up. He's an American worth $480 million.

He doesn't just do books: there's a lot of motivational speaking and workshops. This could be an area that I use to help more people, i.e., make more money.

I go on his website and discover that the workshops have names like "Unleash the power within", "Date with destiny" and "Life and wealth mastery".

This last one catches my eye. Who wouldn't want to master life and wealth? I notice it's a week-long programme in Fiji in October. There's nothing about prices but there is an option on the website to have a live chat with a member of staff. It's just after midday so it'll be very early in the morning in America, but I think I'll try it anyway. I fill in my name and then a note comes up saying, "You are now chatting to Mo Salami."

This is the greatest name ever. I think it's a woman as there's a photo of a pretty blonde lady at the top.

Mo Salami is typing to me now. She writes:

Gooooood afternoon Annabel.

Seriously. There are five "o"s in "good".
I write back:

Hi, Mo Salami, I was wondering about the cost of the 'Life and Wealth Mastery' week in Fiji.

And then because I want her to think I am serious and not a time-waster, I add:

And do you get a free fruit basket in your hotel room?

Mo comes back quickly with the price:

$7,995.

If you can afford this, you do not need a wealth mastery class.
She adds:

Re: the fruit basket, well, that's one I can find out from the hotel. That sounds like a great idea actually.

I'm helping one of the richest self-help gurus!
I reply:

Yes, I love free fruit.

Mo writes:

Absolutely! And that's a pretty great welcome as well, I would say. Carefully selected fruit.

I'm a bit worried that Mo Salami is trying to own my free-fruit-basket idea. But I need to address the money situation.
I write:

Wow, $7,995. I need to go on a wealth mas-tery course to afford this. But at least it's not $8,000.

Mo Salami now types:

> How have you heard about the event and who has
> referred you? And who told you about the fruit?

It can sometimes be hard to infer tone from the written word but I do feel like Mo Salami has turned a bit on me now.

I tell her I was told about the event and referred to the event by the website. And my own brain told me about the fruit but it's often wrong.

Mo writes:

> So will you be joining us in October?

I feel like Mo is trying to get rid of a time-waster.
She does soften it a bit with a follow-up message saying:

> The setting in Fiji is great and little details like the fruit
> certainly can make a difference.

Mo Salami has totally stolen my fruit idea. She adds:

> And of course the programme is phenomenal.

I'm starting to get worried that I'm going to be tricked, using techniques mastered by Tony Robbins, into signing up and paying $7,995.

I reply saying I need to check my bank balance.

One thing is bothering me though. In the photo at the top, the pretty blonde lady is wearing a microphone headset.

I add:

> P.S. Why are you wearing a microphone headset when
> you are just typing?

Mo's answer is:

I type, I talk, it's great.

She starts trying to talk me into cheaper options now, so I say I'll browse the website later as I've got to have a bath.

Mo writes:

Have an outstanding day, Annabel.

Then she immediately hangs up, before I get a chance to reply.

But that's fine as I've learned a lot. I've learned that I can charge $7,995 for a week-long course. So I devise these three courses:

First week of October: Become more successful while you sleep – $7,995

First week of November: Blink your way to more sex – $7,996

First week of December: Get rich by working hard and not spending any money – $7,997

Plus, a free basket of fruit with each one.

All I need to do now is follow the advice of *The Secret* and spend some time really wanting this to happen and then I'll definitely become a billionaire self-help guru.

32

The Challenge:
To debunk a scientific theory

I am not a scientifically minded person. I've never asked why the sky is blue, because if someone told me why, I know the answer would be deathly boring. The only evidence that I've ever studied any science is a GCSE in chemistry. I got a D. But only because there was a lot of multiple choice and I must've been a bit lucky.

I've always thought that scientists are know-it-alls with all those facts and figures and evidence. Boring! I'm quite excited about debunking one of their know-it-all theories.

And it shouldn't be too hard as they certainly don't always get it right.

Look at Sir Isaac Newton. He's known for two of the big theories: gravity and motion. However, he also believed the Bible was one big cryptic code that revealed the future. It was an obsession. His biographer found thousands of papers where he'd written about it and he claimed the code reveals the world will end in 2060. To be fair to Sir Isaac, this could still be true. I'll give him the benefit of the doubt for now.

Pythagoras, of that famous maths theory that I think is something to do with a triangle, also developed a theory that by using mirrors and human blood you can write on the moon. How this would work is as bewildering to me as why you would want to write on the moon. Maybe you could sell advertising if you did the writing big enough.

I look for more proof that these know-it-alls don't know it all and it turns out loads of scientific theories have been debunked. Even one of Einstein's. He had a theory about the universe being static and Edwin Hubble made him look like a jerk by proving it was constantly expanding. But I imagine he had the benefit of his own telescope.

Nobody believes the scientific theory of maternal impression anymore, the theory that a mother's thoughts affect her unborn baby in the womb. For example, they actually believed that in the case of the Elephant Man, his mum had been frightened by an elephant when pregnant. Surely this would then mean that elephants, who are always scared of mice, would be giving birth to mouse-like elephants. If only.

All this previous debunking is making me feel very confident. I just need to choose a theory to pick apart and expose.

I start by looking at all the big main ones. My big problem is that to debunk them, I need to know a bit about them, and as soon as I start reading about relativity, for example, I'm so bored that nothing goes in.

And then it comes to me, a thought I had two weekends ago while watching a David Attenborough thing about insects. I thought, *What's more believable: that a caterpillar turns into a butterfly or that someone once made up that a caterpillar turns into a butterfly and everyone just fell for it?* The latter is much more believable to me. It's just too science fiction that one creature can suddenly transform into another. No other living thing does it so dramatically. A butterfly is a completely different creature. It's got wings, it flies, it's colourful. And if it were possible, why isn't anything else doing it?

So either someone made it up years ago as a joke and everyone fell for it and they forgot to say it wasn't a joke and then died; or someone was writing an educational but fun children's book about a caterpillar but couldn't think of a good ending, so they made up this butterfly thing and *The Very Hungry Caterpillar* was born. They certainly did very well out of it, with 38 million copies sold.

I really think I'm on to something here.

Just look at the whole process. A caterpillar is born and then all it does day and night is eat. Constantly gorging itself. Like someone morbidly obese. And then it just suddenly stops eating, like that's easy. Whereas the £2 billion UK diet industry says not.

Then the caterpillar hangs upside down from a twig and spins a silky cocoon so it can do the transformation inside. Out of view. Very convenient that, doing the metamorphosis hidden. If I said, "Yeah, I can transform into a cat. Just close your eyes for a bit." And then you open them and a cat is there, you'd laugh at me. So why aren't we laughing at these caterpillars and butterflies?

I feel like I've got clear proof now that it's all lies. But how do I get my debunking believed by everyone? What credibility do I have?

Well, I do have some credibility from the fact I once had a science accident. I picked up a tripod that had had a Bunsen burner under it so was very hot. I got a bad burn on my hand, which scarred. I feel very much like Marie Curie who discovered radium but died of radiation exposure. Or Galileo, who used his telescope to stare at the sun too much and blinded himself.

It's clear I've got the war wounds, which give me some credibility, so now I just need to get my thoughts out there. I briefly consider getting some mirrors and human blood and trying to write it on the moon.

Then I remember Dr Ben Goldacre. He's always debunking bad science and he started out with a column in the *Guardian*. It's probably a bit much for me to get a column at this short notice and, I suppose, based on one idea. But there's no reason why I can't get my views on the *Guardian* website.

I go to the science section. There are now lots of subsections so I go to "biology" as that feels like the closest one. Then I find a very recent article that's getting loads of comments. Over 1,000 since it was posted yesterday.

It is about Brian Cox's TV show and evolution. I'm not sure exactly what, as I don't read it; I don't need to. I go straight to the comments, where everyone is getting in a tizz about evolution and write this:

> I think the point that everyone is missing here and the
> thing that nobody is brave enough to talk about, is the
> lie that is metamorphosis. Are we really still believing
> something as ridiculous as a caterpillar turning into
> something completely different – a butterfly? It's a joke.
> It belongs in science fiction. Not science.

My comment blows everyone way. They are stunned by the truth, stunned into silence. Then are busy going off and doing their own research on this revelation, which explains why there were no responses.

That's really exciting but I need now to push my theory even further out there. Where would we be if Charles Darwin had just left his theory of evolution in the comments section of the *Guardian* website beneath an entirely unrelated article?

I decide the best thing to do is make contact with the Society of Biology. Mainly because they've got their own publication, the *Biologist*, where my findings can be on the front cover. Maybe with a mocked-up picture of a caterpillar and butterfly on the stand in a courtroom being cross-examined.

I head off to their offices in London and decide on the way, to avoid looking like someone who has just wandered in off the street, that I'm from the RSRS, the Royal Scientific Research Society, which is entirely made up but sounds really real.

When I arrive I see that it's a building with five other societies so I tell the receptionist I'm from the RSRS and here for the Society of Biology.

"And who exactly are you here to see?" she asks.

"Oh, I don't have a name," I say. "We've just made a new discovery at the RSRS and I was so excited I just rushed straight over!"

This appears to be enough for her to call up and I hear her saying, "I've got a lady here from the RSRS where they've made a new discovery so she rushed over to share it."

There's a pause, where the person on the line is clearly asking a question. Then she says to me, "What's the RSRS?"

I laugh in a way that suggests I think she's joking as everyone's heard of the RSRS; it's like asking what the RAC is.

She looks at me blankly so I tell her it's the Royal Scientific

Research Society. She repeats it on the phone and when she hangs up she tells me somebody's coming down to talk to me.

I wait, feeling so excited about how close I am now to my theory being lauded by the scientific community. Then a man appears who tells me he's something do with marketing. I'm not sure marketing is right – shouldn't it be the chief discoveries officer or something? But we take a seat in reception and I tell this man all about how at the RSRS we've discovered that it's totally made up that a caterpillar turns into a butterfly.

When I finish, he says, "That's a big statement, quite staggering really."

"Yes," I say. "It's incredibly exciting, we've all been led astray all these years."

And then he says, "It's funny as I heard someone on the radio talking about this last night."

I have a moment where I think, *Oh my God, other people think this too. Not just me.*

Before he continues with, "Yeah, on Absolute Radio."

Oh. It was me.

I've got no idea what to do now. I could go, "Right, yes, okay, you've got me there. I'm not really from the RSRS, I'm a radio presenter pretending to have made a scientific discovery."

But that would be mortifying.

I'm just going to have to try and style it out and keep pretending that I am from the RSRS, which turns out to be no less excruciating. As we both know I'm lying but we both carry on with the charade.

I say, "Yeah, I did speak about it on the radio last night; it was great to get that publicity. I also got it in the *Guardian*."

"And what is the RSRS?" he asks me.

I tell him what it stands for but I stumble a bit on the scientific bit. I go to say "society" and have to correct myself. He's smiling broadly at me the whole time.

Then he gives me his card and asks me to email it all to him.

"Will it go in the magazine, then?" I ask. He says he can't promise.

I send him this:

Dear Mark,

Lovely to meet you before. I'm back in the office now, so thought I'd put in writing our remarkable discovery, which would be great to feature in your *Biologist* magazine.

So here at the RSRS, we realised that regarding the phenomenon of caterpillars turning into butterflies, it's actually more believable that somebody made it up than that it actually happens. Let's face it, no other creature does it and it does it hidden from view, like Houdini escaping from padlocked chains when he has actually got the key Sellotaped to the sole of his foot or something. It's not science, it's science fiction. And it's kind of embarrassing that we've believed it for so long. We look like jerks.

But at the Society of Biology you can escape this embarrassment. Please do publish our findings.

Let me know today what your plans are as I've got the *New Scientist* on my back, but I like you more.

Many thanks and all best wishes,

Annabel

I hear back quickly.

Dear Annabel
   Many thanks for your email.
   We've hugely enjoyed your early/late April Fool's joke in the office today. Please feel free to accept the *New Scientist* offer.
   Best wishes
      Mark

I'm a bit confused as it's October and I don't think early or late April Fools are a thing. If you do it outside of 1 April, surely it's just a joke. And I wasn't joking. But the good news is, someone at the Society of Biology clearly listens to the radio show. So maybe other great scientific minds are listening too. I can leave all this in their safe, know-it-all hands.

The End (or why I stopped doing all of this)

This feels like a good place to end. A place where someone has finally exposed me as a radio presenter wasting everyone's time. I suspect it says a lot about our listening figures that it took so long for this to happen. And these are just thirty-two challenges out of around one hundred and eighty that I did. One hundred and eighty over five years. Did I not mention before that I did this for five years?

Now you think I'm insane and Geoff is a sadist. What kept me going though, was the loveliness of others. In my life before these challenges, I'd thought about 15% of people were lovely. I now think it's around 95%. They are far more accepting, tolerant, patient and kind than I ever would've imagined. Or perhaps it's just a politeness that stems from fear: "Yes, I will massage your back in the street but only because, even though you look normal, this is not a normal thing to ask, so I am terrified of you." Maybe that's it. Actually, I'm pretty sure that is it.

Geoff once said to me while setting a challenge, "Things will start going wrong for us at some point. My long-term plan is to become destitute. I see myself as very much going down the tramp route. But I feel somewhat responsible for you. I feel a bit like how Frankenstein must've felt about his monster."

I suppose there is something a bit monstrous about someone unashamedly getting in a sleeping bag in a bar in the Ritz.

And there is still time for us to realise his vision of me, shunned by society, and of him collecting cardboard. The radio show where all this happened is now no more, so these challenges really are over. But if you're ever at work and get a call from reception saying that a Finty Mettledown is here to see you, maybe it's me, doing it all again for old times' sake and because I'm bored of watching television.

About the Author

Annabel Port is a Sony Gold Award-winning radio presenter, formerly of the *Geoff Lloyd with Annabel Port* show on Absolute Radio. She is also a podcaster and has written for television. *Annabel vs the Internet* is her first book.

Acknowledgements

This is going to be very much like an Oscar acceptance speech (but without any of the actual winning of an award). I'm going to really gush, safe in the knowledge that I don't have to have eye contact with anyone while I thank them. Make no mistake about it, I'd never be able to say any of this to their faces.

Firstly, thank you to everyone at Unbound, especially my editors: DeAndra Lupu for whittling and polishing the manuscript into the book you hold now. And Philip Connor for his help shaping a series of radio challenges into something readable, patiently wading through all my bad writing habits and for gently telling me that it's "hang-gliding" not "hand-gliding". Who knew? Not me, as it turns out.

I would also like to thank Danielle Zigner for her input at the very early stages of the book, and Sara Barron for generously giving me unlimited access to her expert opinion and invaluable advice throughout.

I'm indebted to Geoff Lloyd for giving me the opportunity to work on a radio show and the space to learn how to do it. Most importantly, he devised the radio feature and came up with all the challenges you read here as well as countless others. I'm just a workhorse cowering in the glow of his genius. If this was my Oscar speech, I'd probably be crying now.

Everything you've read was originally heard on Absolute Radio so thank you to all the producers that I worked with there during the course of these challenges – Nelson Kumah, Gareth Evans and Dan Benedictus. I'm also very grateful to John Williams and Kiersten Lucas, without whom I would never have had a job there.

The orchestra has probably started up to try and cut me off now but I can't finish without acknowledging the unnamed and much appreciated real-life cast of this book. The security guard at the Ritz, the youth-club worker willing to believe I was seventeen, the man on the street who let me try out metempsychosis, and every other person I approached who was patient and kind, tolerating my ridiculous requests and replying to my stupid emails. You cheered me up every workday and made me like people more than I ever used to. I'm sorry for wasting your time.

To the crowd that funded this book, without you this would still just be a dream. I want you to feel like a big Daddy Warbucks-style benefactor for the rest of your life.

And finally, thank you to Tom. For everything else. Even though you *still* haven't finished reading the first draft. I haven't taken it personally.

Supporters

Unbound is a new kind of publishing house. Our books are funded directly by readers. This was a very popular idea during the late eighteenth and early nineteenth centuries. Now we have revived it for the internet age. It allows authors to write the books they really want to write and readers to support the books they would most like to see published.

The names listed below are of readers who have pledged their support and made this book happen. If you'd like to join them, visit www.unbound.com.

@RoyalGallon
Jude Abeki
Nicole Adams
Polly Adams
Spiros Adams-Florou
Edward Adkins
Rebecca Alder
Juliette Aldous
Alison Alexander
Cameron Algie
Jasmine Allodi

Keeley Ambrose
Duncan Amey
Lindsay Anderson
Sally Anderson
Colin Anderton
Ashley Anwiler
Llia Apostolou
Carmen Arico
Roberto Arico
Britt Arrand
Sarah Ashraf

Sarah Astbury
Miles Atkinson
Christopher Austin
Suzanne Azzopardi
Helen Bacon
Elspeth Badger
Stephen Bagwell
Ruth Baker
Sarah Baker
Jeff Bamford
Bangerturner
Ross Barber-Smith
Corinne Barker
Simon Barker
Mark Barlow
Ross Barnard
Annika Barnett
Lynn Barron
Thomas Bassett
Stephen Bealey
Naomi Beaumont
Fernando Becker
Pete Beckley
Tristan Beer
Dominic Beesley
Joseph Begley
Adrian Belcher
Leigh Bellinger
Daniel Benedictus
Ed Bennett
Monika Berberich
Louise Berry
Laura Bill

Gemma Bilton
Zena Birch
Carolyn Birkbeck
Holly Bishop
Mariana Bit
Maria Blakemore
Joe Blakk
Andy Bleakley
Chloe Bloomfield
Graham Blue
Phil Blyghton
Rowan Bolton
Charles Boot
Patrick Bos
Karen Bottomley-Wise
Adam Bowie
Lynne Bown
Nick Bradbury
Graham Brant
Jeremy Brent
Guy Brett
Terry Brett
Adrian Briggs
Sean Briscomb
Viviana Briseño
James Bristow
Kevin Brooker
Jules Brosnan
Louise Brown
Mark Brown
David Bruce
Louise Bullen
Neil Bunting

Andrew Burdett
Greg Burke
Andy Bush
Melissa Butler
Ed Byrne
Ben Cadwallader
Ash Caffery
Kathy Calmejane
Anna Cameron
Ani Cammack
Cathy Campbell
Matthew Cand
Melanie Cantor
Eloise Carr
Claire Carter
Alison Cassidy
Jonathan Chan
Sharath Chandra
Michael Check
Greg Cheesman
Laura Church
Heather Churnside
Claire Cinnamond
Dino Ciorra
Michele Clapham
Sarah Clarke
Thomas Clarke
Tom Clay
Emily Coates
Matthew Cocking
Michelle Pelta Cohen
Robert Cole
Katherine Conlon

Kevin Connolly
Cheryl Connor
Aaron Cook
Laura Cook
Paul Cooke
Sandra Copson
Danny Copues
Deb Cornish
Emma Corsham
Gemma Cowan
Matthew Cowan
John Crawford
James Cridland
James Croall
Paul Cronin
Joe Crook
Rachel Cross
Janet Cue
Elizabeth Cullen
Anna Culley
Fiona Cummins
Katy Cusack
Marcus Daborn
Jennifer Dady
Sally Dady
Ivana Damant
Ceri Daniels
Garrie Darling
Sandra Davey
Menna Davies
Sarah Davis
Tania Dawson
James Deacon

Emily Dean

Michael Dean

Robert Dedus

Jon Deeming

Philip Dell'Isola

Claire Denton

Rebecca Devlin

Joe Dixon

Sally Dobbins

Amanda Docherty

Pete Donaldson

Jenny Doyne

Louise Driver

Sarah Dudley

Frances Duffell

Matthew Duncan

Nicola Durcan

Lawrence Dwane

Pete Dyson

Laura Echols

Rob Edwards

Tim Elkington

Thomas Elliott

Daniel Ellis

Paul Elms

Abigail Evans

Gareth Evans

Sam Evans

Victoria Evans

Bob Farley

Cathy Farrell

Lucy Farren

John Farrer

Sarah Fellows

Laura Fergus

Steve Ferguson

James Fidler

Helen Fielding

James Firebrace

Chris Fishbourne

Andrew Fishpool

Martin Fitzgerald

Kim Fitzpatrick

Nick Folwell

Ben Foote

Andrew Forth

Katie Fosberry

Alex Foster

Jo Foster

Martyn Fox

Mal & Tiff Franks

Jamie Freeman

Timothy Frost

Jim Galbraith

Pete Gardiner

Emma Gardner

Tracy & Mark Garner

Eleanor Garth

Debbie Gasho

Joseph Gauci

Eian Gault

Aimee-Marie Gedge

Caroline Gerrard

Mark Gibling

Jennie Gilpin

Stefica Krajacic Gimenez

Ravi Godbole

Pauline Godfrey

Sara Gollom

David Good

Alex Goodyear

Dave Gorman

Deborah Goulding

Annette Graham-Wood

James Grant

Sam George Green

Michael Greenspan

Mark Gregersen

Heather Greig

Shaun Guppy

Grant Gushlow

Chris Hall

Joe Hall

Samantha Hall

Rob Halloway

Stephen Ham

Gary Hamilton

Edward Hancox

Ben Handy

Will Hann

Kate Harbottle-Joyce

Nicola Harding

Ben Hardwick

Kathryn Harker

Pat Harkin

James Harris

Andrew Hart

Victoria Hartley

Erica Hartmann

Graham Hastings

Folly Haulks

Kayo Hayakawa

Lee Hayward

Alan Hazlie

Alexandra Heavyside

Jo Hemmings

Nicola Henderson

Siobhan Hennessy

Michael Henning

Louise Hepburn

Frances Herford

Stuart Heritage

Robert Hibbert

Janet Hindle

Benjamin Hodgson

Alison Hogg

Kurt Hohensee

George Hollingdale

Michael Holt

Damien Hopkins

Thomas Horne

Philippa Hornsby

Ian Howard

Bruce Hughes

Kevin Hughes

Becci Hull

Stephen Humphreys

Chris Humphris

Tony Hunt

John Hutchison

Sam Ilsley

Henley Indge

Fred Inglis

Laura Ipsum

Lee Israel

Mark Izzard

Deborah Jackson

Lee Jackson

Rosie Jamieson

Brian Jeffers

Michelle Jenks

Rebecca Jewell

Joanne - Happy Birthday lovely,

Bear xxx

Kelly Johnson

Michelle Johnson

Rosanne Johnston

Gareth Jones

Gareth William Edward Jones

Richard Jones

Tessa Jones

xxCathy Jonesxx

Ellen Jurczak

Sue Karlstrom

Kay, Isobel and Tim

Amanda Keen

Michael Keen

Anthony Kelly

Beth Kelly

David Kelly

Adam Kennedy

Dan Kieran

Natalie Kinsey

Ali Kirk

Becky Kirk

Charlie Kirk

Daniel Kirkdorffer

John Korzelius

Jan Kozusnik

Zuzi Kubinska

Sanda Kurtz

Anne Lam

Tom Lamparter

Maggie Langer

Christian Le Moignan

Al Lee

Amy Lee

Christine Lee

Philippa Leguen de Lacroix and
    her sidekick Wardy

Ian Leigh

Mimi Leighton

Tracey Leitch

Ivan Levene

Sophie Lewis

Verity Lewis

Tobias Ling

Stephanie Lister

Diane Lloyd

Geoff Lloyd

Scott Lloyd

Stuart Lloyd

Jonathan Lowe

Kiersten Lucas

Ola Lundin

Matthew Lynch

Miranda Mackelworth

Sam Mackeown

Emil Mackey III

Mark Maclean

Martyn Maconachie

Chris Maher

Rob Maiden

Klaus Maier

Eleanor Marshall

Lea Marshall

Brian & Alison Martin

Esther Martin

Paul Martin

Sharon Martin

Marty From New Yawk

Andy Matthews

Despina Mavrou

Andrew May

Sarah Mayhead

Debbie McCaffrey

Alison McCormick

Gerry McCready

Jonathan-Action McCullough

Sam McDonald

Alan McGeer

John A C McGowan

Keith McGregor

Matt McIlroy

Melissa McIlsley

Dawn McKee

Dan McKenna

Jack McLellan

Tony McMahon

Leanna McPherson

Jim McSherry

Sarah Meakes

Paras Mehta

Glyn Mercieca

Marisa Messulam

Craig Brinton Metcalfe

Andy Midwinter

Laura Miles

Ailsa Miller

Jennifer Miller-Childs

Gustavo Miranda

Roxanne Misir

Peter Miskelly

Sarah Mitchell

John Mitchinson

Zoe Molloy

Declan Moodie

Kam Moodley

Robin Moore

Susan Moore

Anthony Moorey

Grace Mooring and Tom Triggs

Theresa Mordan

Rhys Morgan

Sarah Morley

Kelly Morris

Allan Morrison

Sally Morson

Jonathan Morton

Anthony Muldoon

Kyle Mullaney

Shaun Mumford

Brian Murphy

Emma Murphy

Jo Murray

Richard Murray

Sean Murray

Jun Nakamaru-Pinder

Carlo Navato

Adam Neale

Paul Newbegin

Evelyn Newby

Lisa Newman-Hall

Rosanna Ng

Rebecca Nicholas

Todd Nishida

Gavin Noble

Jilly Noble

Rachel Norman

Alexander Northwood

Simon Nurse

Anthony NW

Katriona O'Connor

Paul O'Connor

Alice O'Neill

Adrian Oates

James Obrien

Jason Offer

Joanna Oldham

Siusan Orlovsky

Arran Osborne

John Osborne

Matt Owen

Bethany Packwood

Chris Paffett

Joanne Parker

Jonathan Parrett

Amanda Parry

Matthew Parry

Matt Patrick

Emma Patten

Rob Patterson

Michelle Patzlaff

Claire Pearce

Mark Penman

Paula Perkins

Chris Perry

Will Pethen

Mark Petrie

Andy Phelan

Martin Phillips

Paula Phipps

Sam Pickering

J Mark Pim

Justin Pollard

Robin Port

Craig Porter

Rachael Potter

Graeme Powell

Ian Powell

Emily Power

Michelle Pressland

Colin Preston

Lawrence Pretty

Lauren Price

Cheryl Prowell

Ian Prowell

Idzi Pszenicki

Natasha Pszenicki

Alex Pugh (First Aider)

Alex Pugh Ba Hons

Grant & Becky Pye

James Radcliffe

Jenny Radley-Phillips

Danny Raffwood

Desmond Ramzan

Mike Redmond

Barry Rees

Carly Reid

Paul Renwick

Stephanie Ressort

Lindsay Richards

Ian Richardson

John Richardson

Mary Richardson

Tom Richardson

Kirsty Richings

Matt Rickard

Ellie Ridgeway

Peter Rigsby

John Riley

Juliet Riley

Andrew Ringrose

Tracy Risby

Andrew Roberts

Richard Roberts

Claire Robinson

Jayne Robinson

Joanna Robinson

Becky Roehl

Scott Roffey

Duncan Rogers

Miss Sally Rogers

Susan Rollinson

Sam Ross

Davina Ross-Anderson

Jo Rothwell

Benjamin Russell

Chris Russell

Marc & Nanda Rust

Andrew Rutland

Brigid Ryan

Zoe Ryan

Julie Salt

Vickie Sargeant

James Sassak

Natasha Saunders

Phil Sawyer

Katie Scholefield

Stewart Scott

Ian Sealy

Dipesh Shah

Moin Shaikh

Sarah Sharma

Lizzie Sharp

Saffron Sharp

Samantha Shaw

Martin Shelley

Sophie Shorland

Sharon Simcock

Louise Simkins

Vicki Sizer

Clare Skea

Joanne Last Slawson

Shell Smart

Alana Smith

Chris Smith

Christian Smith

Christopher Smith

Karen Elizabeth Smith

Nicola Smith

Richard Smith

Mo Smyth

Nat Snell

Martijn Sollman

Andrew Sparkes

Hetty Sparkles

Carl Spurling

Vanessa Stamp

Adam Stanley

Omeed Starmer

Daniel Steele

Mathew Stephenson

Oliver Stew

Sarah Steward

Joseph Stolerman

James Stone

Rod and Sue Stone

Andrew Stuart

Claire Sturgess

Ben Szymanski

Raymond Tang

Holly Tasker

Chris Taylor

Claire Taylor

Sean Taylor

Laura Templer

Emily Theobald

Alastair Thomas

Neil Thomas

Molly Thompson

Sarah Helena Thomson

Clare Thorne

Dan Thornton

Elizabeth Tobin

Karl Todd

Lloyd Tranter

James Travis

Natalie Trott

Martin Trotter

Kirsty Turnbull

Chris Turner

Craig Turner

Paul Varela

Rainer Vietze

Elina Viitaniemi

Sonja Vogel

Helen Walker

Stephen Walker

Antony Wallace

Chris Walsh

Phill Warren

Rob Warren

George Watkins

Annie Watts

Simon Watts

Stephen Way

Steve Weaver

Nick Wells

Kay West

Tristan West

Barnaby Weston

Lisa Whaley
George Whitaker
Mike Whitbread
Jeff White
Miranda Whiting
Crispin Wibberley
Michelle Wibberley
Joseph Wicking
Vicki Wild
David Wilkinson
Andy Williams
Daniel Williams
Richard Williams
Ryan Williams
Stuart Williams
Bruce Williamson
Donna Willison
David Wilson

Keith Wilson
Lianne Wisbey
Mark Witkin
Tomek Wojcik
Nicola Wood
Official Tim Wood
Simon Wood
Emma Woodhouse
Chris Woods
Ollie Woods
Anna Wright
Dan Wright
Jeffrey Wruble
Garrick Yates
Chris York
Chris Young
Deborah Zbinden

VIP Faces

A huge thank you to the faces of these supporters.

John Betjeman (and Colin)

Both Paul and I got the "tilt your head" memo

Damo's only got one side

Ethiopian mask, hard hat, Stephen

What a lovely face to get stuck to mine